Advance Praise for *What Does It Matter?*

"This wonderful book is one you will pick up and won't be able to put down! Emma provides practical tools to help you live a balanced and joyful life, so you can get out of your own way, to live a life you love. Emma authentically guides you to use this question 'What Does It Matter?' to calm your stress and inner critic and to empower you to have the courage to act on your answer. I am recommending this book to all of my clients as a brilliant tool to calm your nervous system, to help improve mental and physical health."

—Simoné Laubscher, Founder and Formulator of Rejuv Wellness, Formulator of Welleco for Elle Macpherson

"I wish that I had had this book when I was growing up. Something that would teach me how to think in a rational way but not overly dictatorial and not condescending. It is like a friend telling the reader that life is long and you should do what seems right. If I had it in my power I would make sure everybody would read this book cover to cover, and in that way make the world a better place."

—Howard Moskowitz, Ph.D., Multi-Award-Winning Psychophysicist, CEO, Mind Genomics Associates, Inc.

"From the start to the end of What Does it Matter? the pages are peppered with thought provoking questions, life wisdoms, and meaningful stories. Emma's writing style is accessible yet lyrical, transporting the reader to far flung places and bringing characters to life on every page. I've been lucky enough to encounter Emma's insight firsthand and I'm thrilled to witness it shared in this wonderful book. Emma explains the nuanced implications of what and how to think in a way that enables a more fulfilled life for us all."

—Fiona Murden, Psychologist and Award-Winning Author

"Emma Pears writes with knowledge, passion, and experience. She interweaves these three elements with a central message that is powerful: We can be really strong and influential in how we respond to challenges, difficulties, and experiences generally. This book will help readers to ask questions that will give them some peace and direction. Enjoy the ride."

—Colleen McLaughlin, Emeritus Professor, University of Cambridge

"If you care deeply about having a powerful impact and purposeful influence on those around you then this is a must read book. With a flair of passion and outrageous courage, Emma Pears shares personal examples, wisdom gleaned from others, and sound advice on how to embrace life in a new way of seeing, living, and functioning in our world in this present generation. This book is captivating and inspiring as you explore and understand how this simple yet profound framework "What Does It Matter?" can have a powerful impact on the management of our attitude, diaries, priorities, actions, and responses in seeking to live our lives filled with faith, hope, and love. A timely book for this post-Covid-19 pandemic crisis."

—Commissioner Rosalie Peddle, World President of Women's Ministries, The Salvation Army

"A book that will change your life for the better and help put everything into perspective. An amazing read that will bring tears and laughter as you reflect on your own life when you read it. I wish I had read it thirty years ago."

—Jane Galvin, Managing Director, Financial Services

What Does It Matter?

Live with **Less Stress** and **More Joy**

Emma Pears

Post Hill
PRESS

A POST HILL PRESS BOOK
ISBN: 978-1-63758-548-1
ISBN (eBook): 978-1-63758-549-8

What Does It Matter?:
Live with Less Stress and More Joy
© 2023 by Emma Pears
All Rights Reserved

Cover design by Lloyd Kinsley

Post Hill Press
New York • Nashville
posthillpress.com

Published in the United States of America
2 3 4 5 6 7 8 9 10

For my beautiful Mum, Pauline Hunt.

CONTENTS

PREFACE

....

My Story

There are important things that should consume our energy and other things that really should not. If you're anything like me, you may sometimes get the two muddled, which can take all the fun out of life. If that resonates, then this book is for you.

The question "What Does It Matter?" has been a helpful tool in my everyday life. My university career advisors said they had no idea what to do with me, but that I would find my own way. At the time I was offended and more than a little frustrated, but in hindsight, they were right.

As a working parent, I am continually juggling priorities of attention, admin, and adventure. As an entrepreneur, I have built a business delivering leadership development, training, team building, and innovation strategy. I have served private and public sector clients such as Salesforce, HSBC UK, M&G plc, British Telecom, UK Ministry of Justice, UK National Health Service, and the London Fire Brigade. I have also worked with numerous education establishments and nonprofits like Plan International and The Salvation Army. As a songwriter, I have had to deal with insecurities, failures, and successes, navigating the high and lows of the creative journey, trying to focus more on development than destination. I've worked with artists signed to major music labels and have had songs published and performed across the globe. I have also had too many gut-wrenching "near misses" of success to count. I've dealt with situations such as a global rock star telling me (while I was standing there pregnant) that I should not attend any further sessions or meetings "like that" as I'd never be seen as sexy again.

I have sat on the streets with homeless people and regularly worked in refuges, making tea and conversation. I've needed to muster the courage to walk through a crowd of drunk and drugged men twice my size, some of whom were considerate towards me, some of whom were threatening and aggressive. As a research post-grad, I've sat with my supervisor at the University of Cambridge as we grappled to understand why homeless people were living this way and how we may be able to help them, should they want us to. As a performer and conductor, I have stood backstage in arenas and quieted my mind and heart while ramping up my energy to perform in front of tens of thousands of people. As an ambassador for the charity WeSeeHope, I have celebrated and wept with communities in South Africa ravaged by AIDS.

As a director, I have managed large-scale events for the likes of Sir Tim Rice and have also hosted community singing events and projects in my hometown. I've presented and facilitated in countless situations from executive boardrooms to maximum security prisons. As an executive coach, I find asking, "What Does It Matter?" extremely helpful to my clients as a mining tool, helping them find the treasure and sweep away the trash. As a daughter, wife, sister, and mom, this question has helped me to make choices I don't regret, even when they were difficult or inconvenient. It has also exposed choices I do regret and helped me work out what I would do differently next time.

As an author, I am compelled to write this book because I am committed to helping you in whatever small way I can, and that means more to me than the terrifying prospect of being judged for every word I write. I will be judged, of course, and I've decided I am OK with that because I've asked myself: "What Does It Matter?"

Life is an unpredictable white-water ride of fast currents, beautiful scenery, rocky passageways, and calm waters. "What Does It Matter?" is the simple yet profound framework I use when deciding priorities and managing my emotions. It curates my possessions, directs my diary, and filters my speech.

Why this Book?

One morning I dropped my kids off, went for a run, and battled my way through South London traffic to get to a podcast recording. Running a few minutes late, I had just enough time to nip to the loo and don the "Wonder Woman" T-shirt I'd been handed for a photo shoot. Feeling that Wonder Woman should certainly contest our twinning, I sat down with the host, Cathy. We talked about all sorts of things that morning, but one thing stood out. One thing led me to write this book.

My mom was incredibly laid back, and she raised five daughters. How on earth did she do it? We talked about her advice to me growing up, and there were several gold nuggets, perhaps each one deserving a book of its own. But on that day, one thing she frequently said struck a chord: "What Does It Matter?"

I heard that phrase when we spilled our fruit juice over the table, when we couldn't decide what to wear, or when she was cajoling us not to take ourselves so seriously.

Asking this question provides a welcome and constant pressure release in my own life. I rob stress of its power as I say it out loud. It reminds me that much of what I could feel anxious about is unimportant, and I give myself permission to care less about those things. It also helps me to carve out capacity and give my attention to the people and things I value highly in my life.

This phrase seemed to encourage listeners of the podcast, and I received feedback of how it helped. It continued to gain traction as I learned people were comparing their "What Does It Matter?" stories. One lady, a single mom who is also a full-time social worker, stopped me to say how much it brought her freedom in a particular moment. Life was full-on, and as she said goodbye to her teenage son leaving for school, she realized she hadn't ironed his shirt properly. Previously she would have stressed out, telling herself the story that people would judge her as a single mom, that she was failing and wasn't doing anything right. But in that moment, she heard my mom's wisdom: "What Does It Matter?" She immediately gave herself grace and decided not to be so hard on herself. In that moment she saw the creased shirt for what it was: trivial. The question acted like a pin in the balloon of her increasing anxiety. She managed to stop herself from escalating the minuscule into a mountain.

Another person spoke of deep regret because he prioritized work, missing out on each and every sports day his children had. When he finally decided to go to their sports day, they were adolescents and were embarrassed he'd turned up. They were too old for their dad to be there then; they'd needed him when they were young. His failure to ask himself: "What Does It Matter?" led to disappointment and sadness. He has a relationship with his family, but they're not as close as he'd like. In this scenario he had mistaken the significant for superficial.

This book explores why we make the decisions we make and how we can make better choices in an instant by refusing to overestimate or underestimate the importance of any one moment, incident, person, or circumstance in our lives. I hope it will help you live with more fun and less stress by putting life in perspective.

I recognize what matters to you will be different from what matters to me. Therefore, although I will share my own views, I will not tell you how to live your life or assume what is important to you. I will, though, encourage you to ask the question for yourself. The answer may be different for each of us. What is universal, however, is the need to ask it.

Let's live our days with life itself in perspective.

We are amazing human beings. We owe it to ourselves to ask: "What Does It Matter?"

How this Book Will Benefit You

I've learned how to implement "What Does It Matter?" because I've needed to. I use it to reduce unnecessary stress and am always grateful for the perspective it brings to my thinking, feelings, and actions. I hope this book will help you to enjoy your life more and help you discover deeper meaning for yourself and those you love.

Education and career progression are often funneled into an increasingly narrow specialism the higher you go. Our system suggests that being an expert means knowing everything you can about an extremely small field. If this be the case, I am no expert. I am, though, a generalist whose superpower is the ability to learn from others more expert than I. Taking a wider view, seeing the patterns and connecting the dots enables me to draw conclusions, create frameworks, and build on the knowledge and wisdom of genuine experts in their fields. This book highlights the hard work of scientists, philosophers, psychologists, and theologians who have dedicated their skill and wisdom to understanding humanity and how we relate to the world we live in. I am indebted to them for teaching me.

"What Does It Matter?" is the runway of my approach to people, purchases, problems, and projects. I have used it as a tool to live an exciting, varied, and laid-back life, built on a foundation of values where those around me feel important to me, because they are. Here it is, my authentic self, offering something I have found undeniably helpful in my own life for you to use in yours, however you want to. And the "however you want to" bit is crucial, because the best lesson you can take away from this book is to remember to think before you follow. Remember to think before you overreact. Remember to think before you ignore. Remember to think before being so hard on yourself. Remember to ask: "What Does It Matter?" to help you see the funny side of things sooner. Remember that you are in charge of you, and your life is yours. You can think for yourself, and don't let anyone tell you you can't. Happiness propaganda may communicate you are not enough and your life is substandard, but I hope this book will serve as a direct torpedo hit against that commonplace assault. You are better than some media says you are. Use this book as part of your protection plan against self-destruction, and then use it to help others.

The following pages are structured into seven sections, each addressing key elements to help you live a healthy life, prioritizing what matters to you. We look at our thinking, decision-making, expectations, and how we may use our time, money, and circumstance to our advantage. The aim is to remind you that you are your own responsibility. People who have never met you and who are trying to sell you something do not necessarily know what's best for you. You know what's best for you, but you need to remember to stop and ask. Stop and think for yourself.

Subjects covered in *What Does It Matter?* (*WDIM*) include:

1. WDIM...What I Decide?
2. WDIM...What I Think?
3. WDIM...What I Expect?
4. WDIM...How I See Things?
5. WDIM...How I Spend My Life?
6. WDIM...What I Possess?
7. What Do I Matter?

The WDIM framework will help you to unpack the power of "What Does It Matter?" and this book shows you how to apply it to your life. WDIM involves first naming the situation or your feelings, defining the exact issue, assessing its true importance, and then planning for action. I believe using "What Does It Matter?" will serve you in your pursuit of living life with less stress and more joy.

WHAT DOES IT MATTER?

The following pages include tools to help you manage your:

- Stress
- Anger
- Apathy
- Thinking
- Decision-making
- Fear of missing the better option
- Self-esteem
- Spending
- Expectations
- Hurt
- Anxiety

You will also find encouragement to enhance your:

- Joy
- Love
- Compassion
- Hope
- Peace
- Empathy
- Perspective
- Relationships
- Insight
- Patience
- Fun
- Wisdom
- Freedom

INTRODUCTION

In July of 2018, I sat in a black swivel chair, obeying instructions to sit still, tilt my head, close my eyes, open my eyes, look first at the wall, and then at Amy. It was noisy, and bright white light bounced off mirrored walls with people rushing in and out, eager to be prompt for their call time. Amy regularly did my makeup, and we always enjoyed catching up on each other's news. On this particular day, something she said left me utterly speechless.

Fast forward a few days, and I dialed the number Amy had given me to speak with her husband, Tim. The sixty-year-old Englishman answered with a friendly voice, unsurprised by my call. We exchanged pleasantries, and I asked him to tell me, from his point of view, exactly what had happened.

A few weeks previously, Tim's family was concerned because he was becoming a little forgetful. Nothing major, just a few things here and there, but the pattern of absentmindedness warranted further investigation. He went to his doctor and was deeply reassured when he passed the memory test. Nevertheless, just to be sure they weren't missing anything, his doctor decided to send him for magnetic resonance imaging (MRI). An MRI is a type of scan that uses strong magnetic fields and radio waves to produce detailed images of the inside of the body.[1] The scanner is a large tube that contains powerful magnets. The patient lies down in the tube while the radiographer controls the scanner from a different room. Prior to the scan, the radiographer asked

Tim a series of questions, the last of which was: "Do you have any metal in your body?" Tim mentioned he had a titanium shoulder and no, he definitely did not have any metal in his head. After the scan the medics were, in Tim's words: "miffed."

"You should have told us about the metal in your head!"

"What metal?"

He was stunned. They showed him the images and pointed out the foreign object. He was flabbergasted as he stared at the clump of metal sunken into his skull. It was just off to the right, midway between his eyebrow and crown.

Shocked, he struggled to think. Was there medical history he didn't know about? On the way home from the hospital, he called his wife, my friend Amy. "What?! There's metal in your head? Perhaps you should call your mother to see if she knows anything." So, he did.

"Hi Mom, I've just arrived in from the hospital. I know this may sound crazy, but they've found a metal object in my head."

Her response: "That'll be the bullet, then."

What a line! "That'll be the bullet, then." Calm as anything, that was his mother's response to this astounding discovery.

"What bullet?!"

"When you were seven years old, our neighbor was out shooting rabbits. You were playing in the garden, and a bullet bounced off your head. Well, we thought it did. There was a little blood, but you were fine and continued running around quite happily. We assumed the bullet had scraped you. I didn't take you to hospital and didn't call the police. It was just an accident, and we thought it was a lucky miss." Can you imagine discovering that for fifty-three years you've been walking around with a metal bullet in your head?!

In 1953, a tiny sixty-three-year-old Cree woman by the name of Bella Twin made history when she shot a grizzly bear with one shot from a .22 rimfire rifle, the same model used in the rabbit shooting accident. Like Tim, the bear was shot in the head. Unlike Tim, the world-record grizzly dropped dead on the spot. Seven-year-old Tim hardly noticed.

The doctors followed up with Tim and after further investigation decided to leave the cartridge exactly where it was. It had been there over half a century without causing damage, and they suspected that removing it would be riskier than leaving it in position.

So, Tim is still walking about in the south of England with a bullet in his head, and whenever he says or does anything silly, his family simply responds with: "Oh, that'll be the bullet, then."

What Does It Matter? is a book about finding out what is in your head and how you can use it to your advantage.

Questionable Questions

"I've figured life out. Live the same as me, and you'll be happy." This might have been the title of this book if we all lived the same lives, enjoying the same things. It may even be the subversive title to many social media posts, news stories, self-help books, and marketing campaigns.

My title, though, is a question not an answer. I believe the universal application is in remembering to ask the question, rather than the answer that the question affords. It is in asking the right questions we find wisdom.

For example, if I see a train and give you the opportunity to ask me questions about it, what would you ask? How big is it? How many passengers are there? What is the driver's story? What color is it? Where is it headed? What sights might you see on the journey? What if I told you the train was travelling at 200 mph?

If you discover a train is travelling at 200 mph, the imperative questions are: Where is it and in what direction is it travelling? Why? If it is 200 miles away, no problem. If it is two miles away and heading straight for you, you're in trouble! To ask the right questions at the right time is vital. It would be a mistake to be distracted by other details about the train aside from the one that truly matters: It is hurtling towards you.

I am not an expert on my own life, let alone on yours. So why read this book? I am sick and tired of celebrities and influencers telling me that if only I bought this, did that, and tidied my house in a particular way, my life would be transformed.

What Does It Matter? is an exploration of guiding principles and questions applicable to everyone, while at the same time respecting that we are all unique.

Spot the Difference

Dr. Howard Moskowitz is a psychophysicist who became celebrated the world over when his work was brought to light by author Malcolm Gladwell who said: "That is the final, and I think most beautiful lesson, of Howard Moskowitz: that in embracing the diversity of human beings, we will find a surer way to true happiness."[2]

Howard answered my Zoom call while untangling some complications with his audio. "Hold on" he said, "Can you hear me?" The answer to this was no, not really, but I could hear myself. It was an awkward start to a highly anticipated meeting, well, for me at least. He came in and out of the meeting several times, tried different headsets, and then finally settled on audio only. He is a charming and highly entertaining character. I gave him every ounce of attention I could muster, not wanting to miss a moment of his wisdom. His heavy New York drawl was endearing, and he commented that the only reason he took a meeting with me was to add my extremely "posh" English accent to his list of friends. Howard asked many open-ended questions and genuinely wanted to hear the answers. He was interested in my family and said the most important part of our whole conversation was when I described my husband as kind. "Kind," he said, "is the most important word we've used so far."

He was generous and listened intently to my ideas before he expounded his revolutionary work on Mind Genomics.[3] Back in the 1990s, Howard turned consumer marketing on its head by pointing out that there was not one "perfect" product. If you really wanted to please people, you needed to create many variations of the same product and listen to what people really wanted. People should not only be segmented by demographic but by mindset. Malcolm Gladwell says it best in his TED Talk, "Choice, Happiness and Spaghetti Sauce," so I won't retell the story, but the principle of top-down universal perfectionism is one I want to address in this book.[4] The very idea that one size or one taste fits all has been debunked for a couple of decades, and we are quite used to having choices in the consumer market. That is, except for where happiness is concerned.

I want to draw a parallel between big brands that needed to diversify their products and the happiness propaganda that is prevalent in our society today. We need to diversify the happiness message. Of course, we need to discover fundamental truths that are unchanging, but we also need to allow more margin for the bespoke outworking of those truths. The concept that happiness is just a matter of getting the perfect set of ingredients correct is a lie, and it is a lie repeatedly told by big brands and big media.

This book looks at the universal approach to happiness, both where it works in our favor and where it doesn't. Sure, we need to discover the absolutes, the things that are common across all humanity. We also, though, need to spot the propaganda. Of course, variables don't fit with marketing campaigns that want you to believe if only you did this particular exercise, bought this product, and looked ten years younger, you'd be happy.

How would they sell happiness to us if we realized we had it all along?

I shared my vision with Howard and he agreed, right before he popped out of our meeting briefly to go to the kitchen, shouting over his shoulder: "You know, you never own coffee, you just rent it!"

Chase the Sun

Imagine chasing your shadow around all day. It would constantly move and might be hard to find. Your shadow is elusive and focusing on the ground could leave you confused because it would be there one moment and gone the next. Looking at other people's shadows won't help, either.

The trick to finding your shadow is not to concentrate on the shadow at all. Instead, create the environment conducive to it appearing. Find the sun and your shadow will follow.

Imagine happiness to be a shadow. If you chase the shadow with no thought to the sun, you will end up exhausted, sometimes finding what you're looking for and sometimes not. If, on the other hand, you give your attention to the sun and focus on your environment, your happiness will automatically follow. It will be yours and not someone else's, because all our shadows are unique. Though they may resemble other people's shadows, they will ultimately be our very own. The lessons in this book will help us to stop chasing the shadow of happiness and focus on the sun that creates our unique version of it. There is power in the asking, in the pausing, in reflecting, and in noticing. Search for the sun. Rather than telling you answers, this book explores a question we can all apply so your honest answer will be tailored for you. I do not presume to tell you how to live your life. I am, though, happy to ask questions that enable you to figure it out for yourself.

Underwear Everywhere

I noticed my underwear drawer was messy and made a comparison with a perfectly neat drawer, organized by Marie Kondo, the tidying guru of this century. This moment encapsulates the ridiculous world we live in. When, in history, would people know what each other's underwear drawers looked like? In the Victorian age there were public and private spaces even in the home. The parlor, which was often the front room, was for guests, and the kitchen was for family. Now, it seems everywhere is public. Even if you haven't made everything in your life open to all, others have proffered theirs, and as such you have something with which to draw a comparison.

When I finish a run, my app gives me the option to report my supposed success. It almost infers that if I don't tell everyone about it, its viability is in question. I must specifically select not to share in order to close the app. Of course, I realize there are times when you may be doing a group activity together or when accountability is helpful, but I'd much rather opt in rather than continually opting out. The more public we are with our lives, the more we offer material for competitive comparison, and that operates both for and against us.

How do we step away from the fear of being judged and push back the need to conform? How do we resist the perpetual search for elusive "happiness," which some profess to be "out there" rather than "in here"? Well, we stop and ask ourselves: "What Does It Matter?" and the beautiful thing about asking the question is the variation of answers depending upon your circumstance, values, and personality. The answer may even change from day to day, depending on what else is going on. Something of utmost importance in one moment can dim to insignificance in another.

That's what is wonderfully freeing about the whole thing. What is important to you right now may be different from what is important to you in ten years, and what is important to me may be different from what is important to you.

What we have in common, though, is to live a life we enjoy and don't regret, we need to ask: "What Does It Matter?" regularly. We need to give ourselves a break from unrealistic expectations of how our life should or shouldn't be. We need to be brave.

I needed to run an errand to the post office this week. I could have driven there and back in ten minutes, but I asked, "What Does It Matter?" and that led me to question what I would enjoy. I realized I would appreciate walking there, so I took an hour to do a trip that could have been done in ten minutes. Certainly not the most efficient way of doing the chore, but it was the most pleasurable, and that counts. It counts because I want to relish life.

What makes you feel alive? What brings you enjoyment?

Your life is made up of your everyday choices. Make the most of it. "What Does It Matter?" will help us be honest with ourselves about what we really want. It will help us unearth our priorities. It will help us realize how we will feel about our decisions, not just in the next ten seconds, but in the next ten weeks and perhaps even ten years.

"What Does It Matter?" is not a method of constraint, it is a corridor to a more enjoyable life. Neither is it a "fix-all" solution. Life is messy and can hurt. Asking the right questions can't fix that, but it will help us respond in the best way possible.

Therefore, my humble offering to you is to use this exploration of "What Does It Matter?" to help you figure out what is significant to you. To help you notice who matters to you. To help you find the peace and happiness you crave. To help you make both trivial and gargantuan decisions in a proportionate way.

Live a life you enjoy more with less stress because you remembered to ask yourself: "What Does It Matter?" and had the courage to act on your answer.

What Does It Matter?...
...What I Decide?

IT'S YOUR CHOICE

....

⬤ Get a Grip

I'd worked all day, done the school run, still had to prep for the following day, and my husband had a late engagement at work. The kids were hungry, and I had this weird moment: I couldn't decide what to make them for dinner.

I started to feel my stress levels rise way beyond what was reasonable. We were not under threat and had plenty of food in the kitchen. The issue was neither provision nor safety. My problem was the decision required and the urgency to make it. I was like a rabbit caught in the headlights. What on earth could I make for them? If this seems silly to you, perhaps you have not been a parent running a business while trying to ensure that everyone has everything they need, at the right time, in the right way. Always.

In that ridiculous moment standing in the doorway of our living room, I stopped and took stock. I literally said out loud to myself: "Get a grip, Emma. What does it matter?" Everything crystallized in a flash. I told myself: "Just make sure they have food and are not hungry." I honestly did say this out loud, and the relief was immediate. I felt reassured in the same way a good friend may have helped had they been there with me. Declaring the words and speaking to my stress was powerful! I went into the kitchen and made simple cheese sandwiches. I gave myself grace. On that particular day, the fact that I was there for my children, was present in the moment, and we had food to choose from was enough. And based on what I was doing that week, it was actually pretty spectacular. I felt like I was failing, but I reminded myself everyone was safe. Everyone was fed. Everyone knew they were loved.

I went back to basics and realized we were all OK. "What Does It Matter?" made me realize what we ate didn't matter, that we needed to eat did. And that bit, I nailed.

Should you feed your kids cheese sandwiches every day because it doesn't matter what they eat? No! On occasion when you are under pressure, if life as you planned has happened, but other things you didn't plan have also careered onto your path, if all you can manage is a sandwich, what does it matter? What was I afraid of? What made that decision so stressful?

I think it was because I was trying to "get it right." But what was "right"? Actually, a quick, easy decision by a happy mom was better than an English roast with me stressed. Did my kids care? No. Were they happy they got to eat? Yes.

● Toxic Stress

Dr. Caroline Leaf identifies four reasons why we make bad decisions or find it hard to make decisions at all. They include tiredness, being distracted, extreme emotions, and having too many choices. In that moment I could relate to at least two of those: tiredness and too many choices. She says:

"Too many choices are like surges of energy all hitting the brain and the mind at once in an unfiltered way and can lead to feelings of being overwhelmed and put you into toxic stress.... And in many cases, this can lead to decision-making paralysis where you just don't know what to do, you're just staring at the computer, the page, the person and you just can't think."[5]

I can relate to Dr. Leaf's description of the effect tiredness has on our decision-making: "When you are tired, chemicals don't flow as they should in your brain and the internal networks of the brain can get stuck or over-fire and when that happens you don't think clearly.... This is like driving through torrential rain with broken windscreen wipers. You just can't see what's going on!" I believe in that moment I was driving through torrential rain with broken windscreen wipers! I was overwhelmed and in decision paralysis. I can't always claim to make good decisions, but when listening to Dr. Leaf's advice on what to do in that circumstance, for once, I actually think I got it right. I handled my brain in a helpful way that put me back in charge of my feelings. I talked myself out of the decision-making paralysis by putting the issue into perspective. I addressed myself by name, and this was extremely important. It allowed distance from the problem, enabling me to give myself the advice I might give someone else. I also asked myself a question and paused to answer it. I managed to change gear out of panic mode and into solution mode.

So, what can we do to help ourselves make good decisions when we feel tired or have too many choices in front of us? Well, we start by taking a deep breath, which helps to lower the cortisol levels in our brains. When we do this, we allow our neurotransmitters to flow and help bring order back to our brains. Dr. Leaf says that "by breathing deeply we can help the internal default network of our brains...which are like an orchestra that need to play in tune." She even says that, in her experience, breathing deeply in for four counts, holding for seven, and breathing out for eight helps to control our breathing, which in turn lowers the cortisol levels in our brain.

How marvelous. Choosing to breathe deeply can impact the chemicals in our brain to work for us, not against us. In nineteen counts we can positively impact our brains to help us and lower stress. Imagine what we can do in thirty-eight, fifty-seven, or seventy-six counts! I'm excited about this because I know you, dear reader, are breathing. And I know this because you are reading, which means you're alive, which in turn means that you breathe. All day, every day.

Hoorah for discovering that one solution to those stress-inducing situations is doing something we are already experts at! Well done, us. Now, we just need to remember to actually do it.

Turn Up the Volume

We must also speak out the problem. Speak to yourself, out loud. Tell yourself you will find the solution. When we verbalize something, we not only speak it, we also hear it, and hearing adds to the evidence our brain is accumulating to help us to believe it. I think of it like a court of law, with your brain deciding what it will or will not believe. Perhaps bringing as much evidence into play in as many different forms as possible leads to the conclusion that you truly want to believe, even if at first you doubt. Speak it, hear it, write it, read it. Inform your brain of exactly what you want it to believe. The ensuing feelings and choices may be far better than your first thoughts, which may carry some weight of regret not worth the excess baggage fee.

I definitely helped myself by asking the question: "What Does It Matter?" out loud. It was important to both speak it and hear it. I put the situation into perspective, and that meant it felt like something I could handle more than my emotions at the time were leading me to believe. I could see the issue for what it truly was, pretty insignificant, really. No one else was going to say it for me. It was up to me to say it to myself.

Hit pause on your panic by using the WDIM framework to help guide your thinking in moments of stress.

WHAT DOES IT MATTER?

What	What am I feeling? Notice and name your feelings.
Define	What, exactly, is the real issue?
Importance/ Impact	Ask yourself "What Does It Matter?" Be honest about how important the issue is to you. Think about the real impact.
Make a Plan	Choose to act or to let it go.

Manage Your Stress

Let's revisit my personal catastrophizing moment mentioned above and apply the WDIM model.

What: I stopped, breathed, and noticed I was feeling stressed.

Define: My kids were hungry. I had food but felt stressed and tired, so couldn't decide what to make them.

Importance: It was very important they ate. It mattered less what they ate.

Make a Plan: I made cheese sandwiches and gave myself grace that I would make them something more substantial for their next meal.

Our thinking is attached to our emotions. We are thinking beings, and our thinking leads to our feelings, which lead to our choices. When we manage our thinking better, we can influence our feelings and choices for the better.

Multiple Perspective Advantage

Leaf describes the Multiple Perspective Advantage, which is her term for the unique ability we have as humans to stand back and observe our own thinking, feeling, and choosing.[6] This is also known as metacognition. We can train ourselves to do this, and the positive consequences can be immediate and superbly freeing.

Imagine if the next time your stress levels were rising, you stood back and watched yourself and gave yourself the advice that perhaps you would give your spouse or friend facing the same circumstance. It's easy to see others overreact, assume, and misjudge a situation. What if we asked ourselves the same question we might ask of a friend: "Are you sure? Is that really what they meant? Are you feeling like this because of what happened last week? Maybe you'll feel differently after a snooze or a snack. Don't respond until you know what you're going to say."

Do you ever talk to yourself like this? Talking to oneself in a healthy way can help control our thinking and emotions. It is a tool that can be used wisely to get the most out of the magnificent creation that is our body, including our brain.

10:10

Another technique that helps is asking myself, "Will I remember this in ten hours, ten days, ten weeks, or ten years? What would I say to myself in ten years about the decision I'm making in the next ten minutes?" It puts things into perspective pretty quickly when you think about whether it will matter to your future or not. Sometimes it really does matter. Other times it really doesn't. The point is to recognize which is which. I don't know about you, but I couldn't name all the dinners I had two weeks ago, let alone what I ate six months ago. And yet, did I allow any of those decisions to claim more real estate in my mind than was helpful? Probably.

● Oh, Blast!

Psychologists often frame the reasons we might make bad decisions or act in a way we will later regret into a helpful acronym: BLAST. They say that Boredom, Loneliness, Agitation, Stress, and Tiredness are all states of mind that may lead to making a bad choice. Many of us feel at least one of these things or a mixture of these things on a regular basis.

● I Wonder?

Some circumstances are in our control. If you are bored, find something new that you've never done before. Remind yourself how exciting it can be to learn a new skill or just play and have fun. I am insatiably curious. I scour a menu for a dish I've never eaten before. I look to take a different route than the one I took last time. I love a plan but hate routine. I thrive on new sounds, new people, new experiences, and new places.

I ran my first half-marathon by accident because while out for my short run one morning I thought: "I wonder what a half-marathon feels like? I've never done that before. I don't need to be home for anything, so I'll just keep going and see what it feels like!" Curiosity led me to run over thirteen miles. No one else was with me. No one else even knew I was doing it. There was no applause or sponsorship. I genuinely wanted to know what it felt like! I rarely get bored. My curiosity would not allow it.

Not Alone in Being Lonely

Loneliness is prevalent, and it has increased as we've needed to embrace virtual living and working. Experiencing loneliness is extremely difficult, and it is important to get proactive combating it. Research shows that loneliness negatively impacts our brain development and even leads to a shorter lifespan.[7] If you feel lonely, place yourself where you are not only among other people, but where you need to converse and connect. Choose to go to the checkout with an actual human being rather than the automated one, use eye contact, and ask them how their day has been. It's amazing how even little interactions with people all add up.

I find it helpful to revisit the same places. I often work remotely in cafes and busy spaces to avoid feeling like I'm in a vacuum. It is easy to forget the world is moving with people "out there" when I am "in here" working in silence and solitude. By visiting the same places regularly, I begin to build connection with the people serving and other cafe users. I remember the names of baristas, and when there is a lull, I take the opportunity to ask them how they are. You may find it difficult to strike up conversation, but you don't need to be an extrovert. In these circumstances, it's easier than ever. Interaction is necessary to being served, so choose to use that interaction to spark a conversation, and you both may benefit.

Of course, these everyday shallow interactions are only one piece of the puzzle when needing to build a lifestyle that combats loneliness. We also need deeper and more meaningful connections with people who really matter to us.

Connection Not Just Communication

It is true, of course, that these two things are not mutually exclusive, but neither are they automatic when put into practice. There are too many relationships where

> We are wired for connection, not just communication.

communication is failing and too many communications that fail to enhance relationship.

We are living in a generation that is more connected, yet more lonely, than ever before. Maybe we need to look at the connections we have and wonder if they are connections at all. Maybe the weighting lies more in communication than connection.

Communication can be efficient, but is it sufficient? Loneliness can lead to all sorts of bad decisions and wrong thinking. Let's ensure we help each other not be lonely.

● Get Moving

If you are agitated or stressed, maybe try to do some exercise. You might not want to, but most people I speak to are glad they did. The oxygen rush feels great. Do exercise that works for you, though. You don't need to swim if you hate swimming. I don't really like swimming. I find the concept of strangers bathing together baffling, and I am not reassured that the solution to sharing the same water is to add chemicals. If you ever see me in a pool, know I am there reluctantly! I love running, but you shouldn't feel the need to run just because that works for me. Find what works for you. The universal truth is that moving our bodies makes us feel good. I'm not telling you how to move your body—that's up to you. What works for your environment, your lifestyle, your timetable, your body? If you enjoy bathing in a pool of chemicals with semi-naked strangers, you go for it!

If you're tired, go to bed earlier or find ways to improve the sleep you are getting so it is more regenerative. How we treat our bodies and mental health is

We are our own responsibility.

up to us. We cannot starve ourselves of good nutrients, overindulge on the bad, and then expect our brains to function at their best. We cannot control everything, but we can, as far as possible, set ourselves up for a win.

The National Health Service (NHS) in the UK suggests five steps to improve mental health and well-being. These include connecting with others, being active, keeping learning, giving to others, and being mindful. It strikes me that these are vaccinations against the states of mind that psychologists identify as potentially leading to bad decisions. There are many activities you could do that address more than one of those things at once. For example, singing in a community choir or playing sports as part of a club.

We should look after things that are important to us. You are important. You are an amazing creation, and you can lead a significant, full life. Invest your time into caring for yourself and reap the rewards. Who would choose to leave such a wonderfully made being without its needs met? You need rest. You need people. You need to move your body, and you need to be a learner. If you give your brain and body what they need, it will more likely lead you to a life of health. Looking after your well-being is not optional. You're better than that.

If when reflecting on this you find you are not doing any of the things mentioned here, can I implore you to choose just one you can do today? I believe your life is worth the investment.

Your Journey to Better Well-Being: Choose Your Ride!

Mindfulness: Notice. Take a moment to pause. Notice your environment. Notice your breathing. Notice your feelings. Notice your physical response to your emotions.

Community: A sense of belonging. Sometimes I don't feel like getting out of the house to go to a group activity. Mostly, though, I am glad I did. I leave feeling better than when I arrived. You don't need to be an extrovert for this to apply. People need people. Find your community. If you can't find one, create one. It could be anything from a book club to walking group. Perhaps base it on shared interests or geography. Could you create a coffee morning for everyone on your street? Make the effort, you'll be glad you did.

 Generosity: Humans are hardwired for generosity. Studies have shown that we lean more towards giving than selfishness. When we are operating at our optimum design by being generous, we feel good. This could be giving financially or giving our time. It could be mowing a neighbor's lawn or donating some money. The point is, helping people creates a bridge for the social connection we crave.

 Exercise: Moving your body is good for your mental health as well as your physical health. It reduces the chemicals in your brain that make you feel stressed or anxious and increases those that lead to a feeling of pleasure.

 Learn: Allow your curiosity to show you what you might want to learn. It is difficult to be a beginner again, which is partly why adults spend so much time operating in their comfort zones, only doing what they know they are good at. Be brave and be a beginner again. You'll feel better as you learn.

Decision-Making and Grief

When I experienced profound grief, decision-making was very difficult. I felt disorientated and unable to make even the simplest of decisions when I was in the tumultuous early stages of loss. I remember a great friend turning up at my door with a supply of meals. I cannot express how grateful I was. That small act brought with it large love.

Since then, when people I know are crawling through the arduous terrain of grief, I try to reach out and take some decision-making off their shoulders. At some point, it hits us: "What's the point?" It feels like nothing really matters anymore.

Significant life events can change our mode of operating and interrupt our natural rhythm. At times like these it is still good to ask: "What Does It Matter?" Our answers may have altered as our circumstances influence our perspective, but it is still healthy to name how we are feeling and what truly matters to us in that moment.

Everyday Decisions

Aside from life-changing circumstances, we all still have multiple minor decisions to make in our everyday lives. So how do we push past those "don't know what to do" moments? Those incidents or choices that temporarily hit pause on our flow. Those moments that cause shallow arguments and bickering about what should be done. How do you navigate things that escalate beyond their true importance? What do you do when caught trying to make a seemingly irrelevant and unimportant decision that takes way too long and consumes too much energy?

The Contingency

I have two systems in my life that have considerably reduced my stress levels. The first system that helps me is what I call "The Contingency." Make a plan B so you aren't left high and dry if plan A wasn't ideal. This works especially well if you don't have all the information you need at hand, or if there isn't a right or wrong answer.

When my business started to thrive and moved from costing us, to actually making a profit, my husband wanted to treat me to celebrate. (Always look for opportunities to do that by the way; celebration is widely undervalued.) Rather than ask for a new handbag or shoes, I asked for gym membership. I was shaking as I handed over the card details and committed to a year of paying a monthly fee because I was battling these thoughts:

1. "I don't deserve this."
2. "This money could be spent on more important things than me."
3. "What if I never use it?"

Of course, this thinking was crooked because:

1. What is a better investment than your physical and mental health?
2. It was a reward for working hard and seeing some success (after several failures).
3. It was in my control as to whether I used it or not, so I'd better just use it!

All my reservations could be answered if I only stopped to think about them for a moment. I joined the gym, love it, and use it frequently.

I see regular members and visiting day spa guests on a day-to-day basis. This latter group of people supply me with never-ending entertainment and I remember a heated debate between two women in the changing room. On arrival they had been given a bathrobe, towel, bottle of water, and slippers. They were also given a bag in which they could take anything they wanted poolside. Whether to wear the slippers or not escalated into a monumental issue for them. Now, before you judge these women, just take a moment to think of when you may have done a similar thing—do we take a packed lunch or buy it there? What should I wear to the party? And so on. You know the debate, either with yourself or with somebody else.

Anyway, back to these ladies. They spent a good ten minutes getting all flustered about what was the "right" thing to do. They started asking for advice around the changing room and garnering opinion relating to their dilemma. I am tempted to continue typing this inane narrative just to give you the feeling of frustration that was increasing between them, but I won't. The changing rooms were thirty seconds away from the pool, literally! What if they had put the "contingency plan" into action? What if they had simply worn their slippers and decided if they didn't want them, they could put them in their bag or take them back?

You see, to create a plan to cope with "getting it wrong" would have been far quicker and less energy-draining than the debate raging in an effort to "get it right." And what is right, anyhow?! They wasted precious minutes indulging worry over something that, honestly, in the big scheme of things, really didn't matter. I don't judge them for it; I've done it myself. What led to wasting far too many treasured minutes of their special spa day on such a minor decision? I believe it was a desire to get it "right" but working without all the relevant information.

Can I implore you that when you find yourself in a small decision-making situation where you don't have all the facts, just take a moment to think whether a contingency plan could alleviate the frustration. If one of them had simply said: "Let's take the slippers and see. If we don't want them, we can bring them back or pop them in the bag," it would have been done, and all of us would have benefitted from the lack of drama! The ladies didn't realize the changing room was less than a one-minute walk from the pool. They spent more time debating whether to take the slippers or not, than they would have, walking back and forth with and without the slippers ten times over!

Another good example of putting this contingency plan into action was at my daughter's school choir performance. There had been some confusion as to whether long or short socks needed to be worn. You can laugh at how ridiculous this issue is, but to a nine-year-old girl standing alongside her friend to perform, it is important; she wants to be wearing the correct socks! I decided to put my daughter in long socks and pop the short ones in my handbag. I also took spares for any other parents caught out. Sure enough, one of the girls came in sobbing. She had, after a "vigorous debate" with her mom, decided on the wrong socks. She was upset and so was her mom. I said I had spares, and it was all resolved. Her mom said to me: "Of course! Why didn't I think of that? I could have simply brought the other option along with me, and a whole lot of stress could have been avoided!" There's no judgement from me here. I have wrestled with a decision and, deciding something for better or worse, missed the very obvious option of contingency. Take/wear/do both options, and you know you're covered. Or perhaps, whatever the decision is that you're making just doesn't matter that much!

Help yourself out of indecision by asking, "What Does It Matter?"

⬤ WHAT DOES IT MATTER?

What	What am I feeling? Notice and name your feelings.
Define	What, exactly, is the real issue?
Importance/ Impact	Ask yourself "What Does It Matter?" Be honest about how important the issue is to you. Think about the real impact.
Make a Plan	Choose to act or to let it go.

⬤ Manage Your Indecision

What: Feeling frustrated, unsure what is the right thing to do. Tension building as I try to make the right decision.

Define: I don't know whether to take short or long socks.

Importance/Impact: Seemingly unimportant, but when I notice my daughter's stress level I realize it is important to her.

Make a Plan: I don't know the answer, so rather than opting for one, I take both. That way we are covered. I see my daughter's stress levels lower as she realizes she will not be embarrassed as we have what we need, whatever the outcome.

Proactively look for the contingency option. Make a swift decision and have a plan B with you to alleviate that nagging feeling that you might have "gotten it wrong" or that you may regret it. We can save ourselves precious minutes and a whole tornado of stress by implementing a contingency and not expecting perfection from ourselves on decisions for which, honestly, we don't have enough information to get "right."

⬤ Worst-Case Scenario?

The second system I use is asking: "What's the worst-case scenario, and how will I deal with it?" I have found this to be an awkward and disturbing yet helpful safety net.

Sometimes I get more worked up over the decision-making process than had I gotten the decision wrong. While something is left undecided, my stress levels rise. I just need to decide and deal with the consequences either way. I know not everyone has the same challenges as me around decision-making. We are all unique. I honestly think, though, we all have this ability to struggle over a decision we need to make, particularly if accounting for the feelings of others and we're conscious that resources, whether money or time, are limited.

When faced with a challenging situation, or waiting for a process to unfold, I ask myself: "What's the worst-case scenario here?" I then follow up: "How would I deal with it if it happens?"

It's a little like exposing an annoying unknown creature that is nagging and causing chaos in the shadows. Bringing it into the light diminishes its stronghold.

> A plan for the worst can take the sting out of the unknown.

When you find you are bigger and stronger than it is, it loses power over you. You are no longer intimidated.

So much frustration and turmoil can arise from feeling out of control. As soon as you face the worst case and plan to deal with it, it helps you feel back in charge. It takes that irritating creature and pummels it to a size you can handle. It can feel overwhelming and unruly if you leave it in the shadows for too long because the longer it stays there, the larger it seems to grow. It feeds on fear and anxiety, draining you of your energy while ramping up its own strength. So be brave, turn on the light, face the worst case, plan how to deal with it, and watch as it loses some of its mastery over your feelings. Often things won't turn out anywhere near as bad as you fear.

I used "Worst-Case Scenario" when my husband and I were travelling to New York for five days. We had waited years for the trip and were super-excited to be going. There was horrendous traffic, and our "close to the airport parking" had a questionable definition of "close." We arrived at the wrong terminal, and on approaching the check-in desk discovered we didn't have the correct visas. To say it was stressful is an understatement. We were frustrated, worried, distressed, embarrassed, and incredulous that due to a string of unforeseen circumstances, we were going to miss our flight. This was a good time to use "Worst-Case Scenario." The worst case was that we missed our flight and needed to buy new tickets. It came down to loss of holiday time and money. This was an unacceptable position for us, and we were upset at the thought of it, but when faced with the worst case, it was easier to deal with, and our stress levels reduced. We could find ways to be thankful it was only money and time and not anything more serious. When faced with the worst case, we were gutted but realistic about our situation. We eventually made our flight, collapsed on our seats, and laughed the shock and stress out of our system. We learned some valuable lessons that day, and we have never missed a flight since.

I had a stupendous experience of an ordinary, everyday life decision gone wrong when I went to see *Later...with Jools Holland*. It is a fantastic music show that is filmed for the BBC, and I was fortunate enough to share the same manager as Jools Holland, which meant I was able to get highly sought-after tickets. As this was my first visit, I called my management company and asked for information: Where I should go, what I should wear, and the like? I was on the guest list, so I didn't receive tickets containing the same information as the rest of the audience. I was told it was fine to wear whatever I wanted, and that as long as I turned up thirty minutes before filming began, I'd be fine.

When I walked into the backstage area where other audience members were waiting, I noticed one blindingly obvious difference between myself and them. They were all dressed in black, and I was dressed from head to toe in white. And I mean, all white. A couple of hundred people all in dark colors, and there I was, shining like the North Star! It became apparent that the filming had come with a stipulation to be dressed in dark colors.

I couldn't have been dressed more inappropriately if I'd tried. No, in fact the only thing worse would have been a white bikini, but the chances of that were pretty slim. I laughed. Everyone laughed. I hid among people wearing black. It was all OK. I felt a little silly, but other than that, it wasn't a big deal.

If you'd told me in advance I would find myself in that situation, I would have anticipated being ashamed and embarrassed. But surprisingly, I was fine. I was trying to impress, but instead stood out as "the one who didn't read the instructions." With no advance warning, I had to deal with it. I did what humans are gifted at doing: I got on with it.

I adapted. I coped. I laughed. I had a story to tell. And every time I've been to the show since, I've worn black.

You're Stronger than You Think

Research shows we are not very good at predicting how we will feel in the future when things don't go our way. We work hard to create comfortable situations and avoid mistakes, but we cope and adapt when things going wrong. Mostly, we cope better than we thought we might and we are more resilient than we give ourselves credit for.

When the Worst Is the Worst

There are, of course, terrible answers to "What's the Worst-Case Scenario?" Perhaps a terminal diagnosis, loss of income, or the devastating loss of a loved one. There are harrowing worst-case scenarios. Scenarios where we simply cannot see how we will cope. We bring them into the light, and we don't like what we see. We're still intimidated.

Life is messy, and if you live long enough, you'll find it can hurt. I'm not suggesting that nothing matters. I'm suggesting we need to recognize what really does matter and what really doesn't. Some worst cases are appalling and should put everything else into perspective.

There are incidents in our lives that force us to stop and to take note. They shove us into a different circumstance, and in doing so, alter our perspective. In these moments, our sense for change is heightened, and the speed of our life feels different. It may be the loss of a loved one, ill health, or shocking news. I believe the coronavirus pandemic of 2019 thrust a traumatic, shared experience of vulnerability upon us. Life as we knew it was on hold or lost, and people were asking what new future they could build. I believe many were asking questions about what really matters to them. What and whom they wanted to protect, and what, if anything, they'd like to change. It was a catastrophic season sparking questions of deep meaning.

How important for us all to ask the right questions. What does it matter? What do I matter? What do they matter? Living in relative security too often gently rocks us to sleep, numbed to the opportunities for change.

I'm not suggesting I have all the answers. Or what matters to me should necessarily matter to you. I am, though, suggesting we need to ask these questions afresh as I observe turmoil over the temporary and indifference to the ideal.

> We choose cautious comfort over courageous consciousness.

Continuing on cruise control on the freeway of life without ever checking we are following the course for our ideal destination would be foolish. Foolish maybe, but easily done. We forget to ask. Forget to check ourselves. The worst case can sometimes be the worst, and that is exactly why we should ask ourselves the question "What Does It Matter?" on a regular basis. Let's get life back in perspective and pull the plug on the rising waters of anxiety. Let's recognize what really does matter and what really doesn't.

Your Brain Is on Your Side

Research shows that the frontal lobe (found in the frontal and upper area of the cortex in our brain) is responsible for carrying out higher mental processes such as thinking, planning, and decision-making. We use it every day to direct our choices and thoughts. One of its roles is as an experience simulator, giving humans the ability to experience something in our minds before doing so in real life. It allows us to think how we may feel in a certain situation and make decisions accordingly. For example, I can simulate how it may feel to celebrate a win on the athletics track, and this in turn may motivate me to get up early in the morning and exercise. Or I can resist temptation when simulating how I might explain my behavior to loved ones and people I know well. If you are tempted to behave in a way you'd be embarrassed about when found out, simulate the uncovering of your secrets to family and friends and allow it to direct your behavior in a way of which you would be proud.

I can also think how good or bad something may taste. When in the Cheesecake Factory in Chicago, it was my simulator that told me I would enjoy what was in front of me. I couldn't wait to tuck in! This simulator is a wonderful mechanism and, when it is working well, it is absolutely to our advantage.

Surprisingly, though, our simulator does not always give us the best information. Something we may predict as being awful and unmanageable can, in fact, be perfectly manageable and pleasing in the long run. How is this possible? Well, Dan Gilbert and his team have discovered what they call an "impact bias."[8] This is the tendency for our simulator to work badly and make you believe that the outcome is more different than in fact it really is. How you predict you will feel in a certain moment of trauma may, after some time has passed, be quite different from how you actually respond.

Synthetic Happiness

Gilbert has, alongside other psychologists and economists, discovered that happiness can be synthesized. We can change our view of the world and, due to this largely unconscious cognitive process, we can feel better about the world in which we find ourselves, even if that wasn't the world we hoped for. This ability to synthesize happiness and be content with where we find ourselves, gives us more control over our own happiness. Happiness is not "out there" to be found. It is a state of seeing and being.

Gilbert says we have a "psychological immune system." This is akin to putting on rose-tinted glasses after the event so you can believe something wasn't actually that bad in the long run. You may even convince yourself that you are better off for that event happening. I find this deeply reassuring. It is comforting to think however things turn out, we will, eventually, find good in it and view it to our advantage. We will cope and probably cope better than we first thought.

> "Natural happiness is what we get when we get what we wanted, and synthetic happiness is what we make when we don't get what we wanted. And in our society, we have a strong belief that synthetic happiness is of an inferior kind.... I want to suggest to you that synthetic happiness is every bit as real and enduring as the kind of happiness you stumble upon when you get exactly what you were aiming for."[9]

...And Relax

So, what does it matter? You will find the good in a situation in the long run. You can find a way to make the present and past work for you and create synthetic happiness even if you didn't get what you really wanted or were aiming for. This takes the pressure off! To put it another way, we are better at handling past disappointments than imagining future ones. Perhaps this is a lesson to focus on today and stop fretting about tomorrow, because when tomorrow is your today, you may find a way to create synthetic happiness and be content.

There is a long-standing paradigm accepted by the scientific community called the "free choice paradigm." This phenomena was first demonstrated experimentally in 1956 by psychologist Jack Brehm when he observed that, when making a choice of home appliance, his participants asserted the appliance they selected was even better, and the rejected option was not that great after all.[10]

Basically, once you've made the decision, you tend to value the one you chose and inflate its benefits, while at the same time devaluing the one you rejected, amplifying its negatives. The free choice paradigm enhances our pleasure with our choices.

Making the choice between two different things can feel uncomfortable to us. Faced with the merits of both, we may struggle to choose when they seem equally justifiable. I know people who are brilliant at researching their purchases. They subscribe to magazines, read reviews, and take options on test runs. They are meticulous, ensuring they have gathered every detail before making their choice. I absolutely see the benefit in this approach, even if it is far outside of my own tendency. Fascinating, though, that based on the free choice paradigm, we will end up preferring whichever we choose anyway.

● Be Pleased That You'll Be Pleased

Humans naturally reduce the tension of making choices by re-evaluating after we've chosen and being even more pleased with our decision. Clever us.

We evaluate. We choose. We re-evaluate in favor of what we have chosen.

This is crucial in exploring "What Does It Matter?" because no matter what choices we make, our brain will find a way of seeing it for the good. Maybe we need to stop stressing so much over getting everything "right" and realize that many choices don't have a right or wrong, they simply have an either/or. Fall into a comfy pillow of reassurance knowing the confusion during the process of choosing (our cognitive dissonance) can be short lived, as our "psychological immune system" will enable us to manage either way. How much time could you buy back if you were not stressing over choices, whether that be which car to buy or what to make for dinner? Could you just decide and allow your brain to do its thing and be happy with it?

My husband, Nik, and I recently spent hours choosing between equally excellent deals on garden furniture. We struggled to commit, and our indecision took some of the joy out of the purchase. A couple of times I asked myself "What Does It Matter?" and it helped. I wish, though, I had remembered the free choice paradigm. This is a classic situation where whatever we chose, we'd be happy in the end. The lack of decision was more tiresome than the regret we might face over our choice.

Of course, there are exceptions to this. You may be thinking: "Hang on, what about that T-shirt I bought the other day? I don't know if I made the right choice. I am still unsure whether to return it and find something better." That is a valid point.

There is one more layer to this fascinating discovery.

To Change or Not to Change

Gilbert conducted a study at Harvard involving students at the university. He created a "photography course" and asked all the students to take twelve pictures of things they wanted as memories of their time at Harvard. For example, their dorm room, their professors, or the grounds. The team asked them to choose two out of the twelve pictures to develop and showed them how to do it. Once they had taken the photographs and developed them, they were then asked which one they would like to give up. The students were told they needed to make a choice. They got to keep one photograph, and the team would keep the other.

There were two conditions to the experiment. In one case, the cohort was told they could keep the picture they had chosen, and the one they had rejected would be shipped off to England. It was irretrievable, and they'd be left with the picture of their choice with no option to change.

The other cohort made their choice and were told they could change their mind in a few days if they wanted. The rejected picture would stay close by and could even be delivered to them if they subsequently wanted to reverse their choice. They were given the option to swap at a later date, should they wish.

The students thought they would probably like the picture they chose a little more than the one they left behind and they did, but only by a small amount. The real difference between the two groups and how much they still liked their picture five days later was in whether they were able to subsequently swap it or not. The people who were able to swap their picture were unhappier than those who were stuck with the one they chose. The team concluded that the reversible condition (where they could change their mind) was not conducive to the synthesis of happiness. Let that sink in for a minute.

The last piece of the experiment involved inviting another cohort of students to do the same thing, except this time they were told in advance which option they would like: to be given the freedom to change their mind later (the reversible condition), or to stick with the choice they made in the first instance and not have the option for change (the irreversible condition). Sixty-six percent of people chose to be given the choice to swap! Sixty-six percent of people chose the condition that would make them less happy. This tells us their simulators were wrong. They thought being given the chance to swap would enhance their happiness, but in fact, during the experiment, the Harvard team learned that creating an irreversible condition leads to greater happiness.

> Irreversible commitment leads to a greater sense of happiness in the long run.

The belief that the freedom to change our mind is the preferred option permeates all areas of life from relationships to purchases. It is a mistake to think the less commitment we make, the happier we will be. In fact, we actually increase our turmoil over the decision when we see an option to reverse it.

Good News

I find the theory that we can subconsciously manufacture our happiness to fit with our experience both freeing and reassuring. If we fail to get the job we applied for, a little while after, we may see it as a good thing. We may minimize the positive things about the job and maximize the negatives, while at the same time focusing on the good of staying where we are. It may not feel like it at the time, but our brains will manufacture synthetic happiness to the degree that although the outcome may not be our preferred one in the moment, we will make it so retrospectively. Perhaps this is part of the underlying science behind that old adage "time heals."

Contentment Superpower

Human beings are amazing creations able to adapt, grow, change, and thrive in the toughest of circumstances. Our ability to synthesize happiness and be content with our choices, particularly when they are irreversible, seems to me to be an underrated superpower.

Surely, we can reduce the simulated magnitude of decisions by putting them in perspective, knowing once we have made the choice, we will find a way to be happy with it. And the less reversible the choice, the happier we'll be. It's not that everyone is always happy with everything they decide, but the ability to change our mind wouldn't have made it any better. Asking "What Does It Matter?" helps us to do this.

You can be happy either way

WHAT DOES IT MATTER?

What	What am I feeling? Notice and name your feelings.
Define	What, exactly, is the real issue?

Importance/ Impact	Ask yourself "What Does It Matter?" Be honest about how important the issue is to you. Think about the real impact.
Make a Plan	Choose to act or to let it go.

Manage Your "Fear of the Better Option"

What: Nagging feeling I may miss out on the best or not make the best choice possible.

Define: Both options are good. How do I know which I will be happy with?

Importance/Impact: Depends on the circumstance. It is important to choose an irreversible way to maximize your chance of happiness.

Make a Plan: Be sensible and do your research to the best of your ability (if appropriate) and then take the pressure off. You can create synthetic happiness, so either way you can be happy with your choice.

It is a complex area still under investigation. Our brains are spectacular, and scientists are still discovering how they operate. There are many variables when considering our choices and decisions. What I would say, though, is that asking "What Does It Matter?" may buy us time to remember making an irreversible decision will make us happier than if we could change our mind. It may pause our panic just enough to remember the free choice paradigm (we will re-evaluate to our advantage at a later date) will help us find happiness, whether that be synthetic or not.

Do Your Best and Let Your Brain Do the Rest

So, take the pressure off. Your brain is on your side. It is working consciously and subconsciously for your good. It wants you to survive and thrive and will do all it can to help you.

Make decisions. Commit. Don't exaggerate the importance of things that are not fundamental to your well-being. Do your best. Find rest. Focus on today because worrying about tomorrow will make no difference to tomorrow at all.

What Does It Matter?...
...What I Think?

WHERE'S YOUR HEAD AT?

. . . .

Two Rivers

In the spring of 1999, I swapped my sparkling new engagement ring for a more unassuming one, tearfully kissed my family goodbye, and headed to Russia with five others. I was excited to be going. I love adventure, new sights, sounds, tastes, and smells, and I thrive being in the company of friends. The only downside was leaving Nik, my handsome new fiancé, knowing that communication would be tricky for the month we were apart.

I was part of The Salvation Army, and we were heading to Moscow and subsequently further south through Russia. I volunteered my time to run a performing arts team while at the same time developing my character and learning leadership skills firsthand from some of the best human beings I've ever met.

Towards the end of the trip, we were taken to Rostov-on-Don, where we stayed with remarkable, generous, and kind people. I became accustomed to taking cold baths and eating sardines served on plates of cut-out squares from plastic bags. I observed people with so little, giving so much, and I was forever changed. I was humbled by a wedding gift of a samovar (a traditional urn used for boiling water) from one of our hosts because: "Every family needs one." It cost her an entire month's salary. That samovar still

33

sits proudly on our sideboard and probably always will. It is so much more than a beautifully crafted and elegant appliance. It is a symbol of courage, generosity, and a tender heart.

One of our train journeys though Russia was both exciting and disgusting in equal measure. We felt like children making camp in the living room as we made up the red fold-away bunk beds and set up glasses of black tea and snacks on the table in our cabin. A gold patterned curtain hung from an elastic wire running from left pane to right, about halfway down the large window. It wasn't drafty, so we hooked the curtain over the bed to take in the view. I was thrilled to be in a different environment that was so unlike any train journey I had previously taken. This trip was fun, awkward, and memorable. The toilet was filthy and felt more like a scary ride at a theme park than a convenience. I was sure I could have fallen down the big hole where you could see the tracks running fast beneath you. The corner sink and wash area were exactly how I envisaged they would be in Alcatraz: old, rust stained, unpleasant, and dirty, but functional. Weird as it may sound, I found the assault on my senses rousing. It woke me from the everyday routine of home and added a new color to my life that I was unaware was missing. I had no idea I would thrive in such harsh conditions, but it turned out that firing up my resilience cylinders was beneficial. To hold my breath, cope with grime, and extend the boundaries of my limited comfortable life did me good. In making ourselves uncomfortable, sometimes we make ourselves awake. The discomfort and foreignness of the overnight train awoke me, and I needed that more than I realized.

There were six on our team, all of us from the UK. Partway through the trip we were told we had the privilege of visiting the Caucasus, a mountain range on the south border of Russia. I wasn't entirely sure what to expect and was surprised by the truck that pulled up. I opened the flap of the khaki canvas top and took my place on one of the wooden benches. We crammed in, too close for comfort, and at the sort of proximity that people on public transport in London go to huge lengths to avoid. In London we put bags down, cover seats with coats, and spread ourselves out to make it as awkward as possible for someone to join us. We roll our eyes and tut if a stranger needs the seat, requiring us to sit next to an actual human being rather than a handbag. I remember saying to someone who was apologizing for taking the seat next me: "It's OK, you're more important than my handbag, it can go on the floor!" Those around us looked astonished at the verbalizing of what should have been a given, bar for the majority of people's behavior suggesting otherwise. I choose human over handbag!

Back to the truck. It was extremely uncomfortable, yet kind of fun. Not the sort of thing you do every day, so I embraced the weirdness of it all and tried to communicate with the others who were now, most definitely, in my personal space, and I in theirs. I'm not a great linguist, and even though I had tried hard to engage in the Russian language, all I could say was: "Hello, goodbye, thank you, and ooh, that's very tasty!" Not a super amount of help to fill what turned out to be a full day of travel.

I sensed a change in atmosphere as we approached the border. I sat next to the door, and the group leader told me not to speak. The van came to a halt, and the guard communicated in Russian with those around me. He banged the side of the truck, and we proceeded through the checkpoint. We journeyed along another long stretch before the same thing happened. Again, I was told to be silent. The truck stopped, and a guard stuck his head in and spoke to us. As per my instructions, I didn't reply. There was a little more chat before he, too, banged the side of the truck, and we moved on. It was quite a while after that I became aware of our precarious situation. It turned out just one week previously a group of tourists had been kidnapped and held hostage on the adjacent mountain, just over the valley. Our hosts had been desperate to ensure my enthusiastic and fumbling attempts to communicate didn't land us all in big trouble! We had no idea what we were getting ourselves into. The journey carried on in a relaxed manner, and we continued on our naive and merry way.[11]

On arrival at base camp, we were assigned clothing and supplies for the duration of our time in the mountains. My adopted warm coat was stinky but very welcome, and I was happy to carry my rucksack, even though it went from the top of my head nearly down to my knees. It was enormous, and I walked like a limping camel!

Arthur was a one-toothed, crazy-haired Russian whose kind eyes were set deep within his sharp features. He wore a pale baseball cap, and his skin was creased, framing his reassuring smile. He was experienced, compassionate, and friendly as he sought to look after those in his care. He and his team took pity on me on more than one occasion as they noted my diminutive size in relation to the tent and equipment I was carrying. The mountains were stunning, and the long trek to our first camp was both tiring and inspiring. The air was fresh, the landscape untouched, and scenery so magnificent that I often paused in wonder.

We were trekking along an alarmingly narrow path traversing the mountain when some villagers approached us with horses. While we were all grateful the horses could carry the burden of the luggage for a while, I wasn't entirely sure how to respond when offered a ride. Partly I was over the moon, as I was tired and the opportunity to sit down sounded like heaven. But I was also terrified, as the path we were walking was extremely restricted in places, and I couldn't fathom how the horse would navigate it without sliding down the side of the mountain! The difference between life and death felt as wide as the track, and that was not wide enough for me. In the end I decided the horse was more experienced than me at walking the terrain, so I'd better just trust and get on with it. Arthur and his team walked with us, and the villagers reacted as if they'd seen a circus for the first time. It was hilarious! I had no idea how to ride a horse. I definitely had no idea how to ride a horse on a narrow mountain path. So, I decided to let the horse do its thing, and I tried to stay as still as possible.

The first camp had a fire and some basic cabins. My standard for bathrooms had lowered a little since arriving in this part of Russia, so I wasn't overly fussed about the wooden shack and filthy toilets that faced me. The bunk beds were dreadful, and I dare not think what manner of insects and nature's tiniest beasts were sharing my mattress. We were tired and fell asleep quickly, having laughed our way through the instinctive debrief after a day of adventure.

The next morning, we gathered around the fire for breakfast and to hear where we were headed next. We were going to climb to another camp from which we could reach the glacier. Several ex-military men who had very recently left the armed forces were with us to keep us safe and to help with practicalities. One chap wore a head scarf, open shirt, and constant grin. He took a "special" interest in my friend and me, so we made sure that we weren't on our own at all. To be fair he was the perfect gentleman, just very, very attentive!

The next camp didn't have any facilities at all, and I preferred that. It was better to find somewhere solitary with an awesome view than be stuck in the foul hut we had been using. We made camp and admired the breathtaking scenery. I remember sitting by a river and meditating on a song written by King David circa 1000 BC: "The Lord is my shepherd, I lack nothing. He makes me lie down in green pastures, he leads me beside quiet waters, he refreshes my soul."[12] I was on my own, sitting in a pasture hardly touched by humans, looking up at a mountain with a river running behind me, and I remember inhaling goodness and exhaling peace.

The next trek was long and hot. I was getting hungry, and breathing was a challenge. Arthur walked with me, and at one point, reached up and took a leaf from a tree and ate it. I was both surprised and curious. I realized I'd never seen anyone do that before. He encouraged me to try. I was hungry and thirsty so was willing to give pretty much anything a go. To my delight, it was delicious. The vein of the leaf secreted a sweet liquid not unlike black currant juice. I ate a few more and felt, in that moment, at one with nature like never before.

Arthur bent down with his drinking can and scooped water to drink from the adjacent river. I did the same. It was here, on our knees, he pointed out another river running fast and furiously behind us. I had seen both these rivers at different sides of the camp, and now as we walked towards the glacier, both were in view at the same time. He said it was extremely important to know which river you were drinking from and not to get them mixed up: one would quench your thirst, while the other could make you very sick.

The two rivers both ran alongside our path, and I wasn't always entirely sure which was which, so I followed a simple rule: Where Arthur drank, I drank. What he ate, I ate. I watched this gentle yet tough and experienced man very carefully, as if my life depended on it…because it did.

Two rivers. Two very different consequences.

Two Thoughts

If thoughts were rivers and you were able to choose healthy or unhealthy, what would you do? Do you ever stop to think what you are thinking and whether it is doing you good or harm? You are not your thoughts, and your thoughts are not facts.

Negative thoughts are readily available to us. I can bring situations to mind that I might feel anxious about, or remember people who have hurt me. Easily. Writing this unintentionally does so, and perhaps as you read, it brings circumstances and people to mind for you. Negative thinking does not make us feel good and does not change those things that were said and done. I cannot undo the past, and I cannot control the future. It is normal to feel anxious and stressed. Humanity relies on some level of stress response for survival, but the extent to which our stress is for our benefit or to our detriment is variable.

Negative thinking might not feel like a river running alongside you. It might feel more like a white-water rapid running right through you, perhaps even threatening to sweep you off your feet. But that's exactly it. Let it run through you. Relax. Don't try to find a way around it (exhausting). Don't try to build a dam to stop it (also exhausting). Don't shut your eyes and pretend it's not there (because it really is), and certainly don't kneel and drink from it. Let it run through you. To deny your thoughts and feelings is counterproductive. Recognize them. Declare them out loud and take charge of yourself. Notice your uncomfortable thoughts and refuse to amplify them. Focus your attention on the good river instead. Find it, drink from it, and enjoy its benefits. I can resolve, right now, to think about things that give me hope, such as simple pleasures and friends who make me smile. I can choose to drink from the good river, not the bad.

I watched Arthur, and I drank where he drank. I stayed safe by watching his behavior and letting his experience influence my own. Who are you watching? Is it possible the people who have influenced you may not be choosing a good river for themselves? Perhaps you've witnessed firsthand the freedom of someone close to you taking charge of their own thinking in a healthy way. Or maybe the damage done by unhealthy thinking is very much part of your story. Are you emulating the behavior of those around you? Would it be better to learn from their experience and make different choices?

What does your thinking matter? Well, your thinking influences your feelings. If you are feeling sad, it may be because you are thinking sad. That's healthy to do sometimes, but not all the time. I've heard the phrase "stinking thinking" when referring to toxic thoughts. I'd like to add "drinking stinking thinking" to our vocabulary because, for me, what we think is a little like my choice of drink on the mountain in Russia. Two rivers. One does me good. One does me harm. Two ways of thinking, both readily available. One leads to joy, the other destroys.

What does it matter what you think?

Are you drinking stinking thinking?

Thinking may have seemed inconsequential to you or out of your control, but as with my choice of which river to drink from, the choice is yours.

● Pockets of Memories

We collate experiences as we journey through life. Imagine putting all your hurt, anger, disappointments, and regrets in one pocket as you go along each day. Then suppose you were to take all your joys, victories, celebrations, precious people, happy times, and intimate moments and put them in the other pocket. There is no doubt that they are all in the same coat. They make up part of who we are and how we see the world. Many memories could justifiably fit in both pockets, provoking a mix of emotions. Which pocket do you regularly dip into? Do you reach for the hurtful moments and pull them out for you to relive and for everyone else to see and sympathize?

Sometimes memories just jump out of our pockets and wallop us without our permission. I remember being away with my family skiing, and I suddenly had this huge ache that my mom never met my daughter, and that practically all my mothering years have been without my own mother. I felt a huge amount of pain on my mom's behalf that she was robbed of meeting her grandchildren. Tears quietly streamed down my face, and I simply whispered to my husband that I was having a "grieving day." For whatever reason, that memory, that pain jumped out of my pocket and smacked me in the face. I saw it. I named it. I processed my feelings and put them back in that pocket knowing that grief is part of my journey, not my destination. It is part of who I am, for sure. I held my mother's hand as she breathed her last breath. She was there for my first, and I was there for her last. I remember it and I cry every time.

But when I remember my mom, I choose to dip into the other pocket full of good memories, happy times, and everyday moments of joy. I activate my ability to control my thinking and feelings for good. I choose the good river.

I remember her going down a water slide, except for some reason her bathing suit created so much friction she hardly moved. She ended up pushing, pulling, and struggling her way down while the rest of us watched, doubled over in laughter. She was giggling, aware we were observing from the bottom and that the people behind were waiting their turn. Laughing hysterically, she shunted herself inch by inch down the slide. I can put my hand in my happy memories pocket and think of her coming to sit quietly and listen to me practice the piano or see her doing the ironing when I got home from school. I can remember her dancing rock 'n' roll with my dad or accepting a cup of tea like she was being handed the Crown Jewels. So many good memories. I believe she is honored more by that kind of thinking than ruminating on the trauma and loss.

What do you have in your pockets? What are you pulling out from your experiences? Who or what are you choosing to think about? How does it make you feel? If your thinking is not doing you good, then change it. You can, you know. You are in charge of you.

To control our thinking is a little like using a superpower. You can use it for good or bad. The neural networks in our brain can change through growth and reorganization. What network of thinking are you creating? Giving our attention to something is a little like choosing which river to drink from. We can drink from beneficial things or those that cause us pain. We can focus on life-giving things, helping us to reduce stress. Or we can focus on things that compound our anxiety and lead to insecurity and fear.

If I asked you to name the top three things you worry about, you probably could. For me it would be family health, whether I am making good decisions, and whether I am fulfilling the potential of the life I've been given. You may share some of those worries or you may also add in things like what others think of you, your career, your weight, your aging parents, your visa status, or the upcoming work presentation. We all have different elements of life that have the potential to cause us to worry.

To focus on things that make us worry is one river. It's easy to drink, fast flowing, and readily available. It can be dramatic and get a lot of attention while fueling self-pity and fostering cynicism. Worrying is a little like walking up a downward escalator, though. It consumes a lot of energy but doesn't actually get you anywhere. Often, the things I am tempted to worry about most are actually out of my control. At these times it is important to ask, "What will I gain from worrying if it is out of my control anyway?" Also: "Will it help the situation?"

Decide to Decline

Life continually offers an invitation to worry, which you can choose to accept or decline. The invitation will come because we are human and live in an imperfect world. Perhaps it would do us good to decide in advance of the invitation what our answer will be so we have our response at hand. Even if it be through gritted teeth, a forced smile, and unfathomable courage, we need to refuse worry. Decide to decline the invitation.

The issue we want to worry about will not magically disappear. It will, though, lose some of its destructive power because all that will remain is the true situation and not the imagined, speculative, amplified, or anticipated one.

There is another river, other than worry, available to drink from. A river where you think about all things good, things that are pleasing and honest. People who have done you good and not harm. Eugene H. Peterson writes:

> "Summing it all up, friends, I'd say you'll do best by
> filling your minds and meditating on things true,

noble, reputable, authentic, compelling, gracious—
the best, not the worst; the beautiful, not the ugly;
things to praise, not things to curse."

Philippians 4:8–9 (MSG)

Stop pressing where it hurts! How often do you focus on what you are not worried about? How often do you think of things that could be a worry but aren't?

Attitude of Gratitude

We consciously practice an "attitude of gratitude" in our home. If I wake up concerned or overwhelmed, I start saying things I am grateful for. Don't get me wrong, I am not an angel who finds everything easy, but I can create a list of things to be grateful for in an instant. This helps me focus on what I am not worried about, and in doing that, I realize there is plenty that I could be worrying about but am not. That in turn leads to more gratitude.

There is an old hymn, penned by Johnson Oatman Jr. in 1897, that says to count our blessings one by one. This concept is right up to date with current neuroscience. Gratitude has been practiced for centuries by many people of different religions and faiths—and for good reason. It does our brains good and helps our sense of well-being.

If you are struggling, focus on something good. Practice an attitude of gratitude. Don't overgeneralize to "my life is great," but rather, decide to count the good things one by one. Name the things you are grateful for, one by one. By focusing on good things, our attention is diverted to work for us and not against us.

The more specific the gratitude, the better it is for you. Be thankful for the detail. The same principle applies when I receive gratitude. I am delighted to get a thankyou card with the message: "Thanks for the present." If, though, I receive a card thanking me specifically for some detail, such as the recipient especially loving the color, it feels even better. Generic gratitude can feel a little diluted. This doesn't exempt it from power, but the more specific it is, the more we feel the warm, positive, and pleasing affects. It may take increased effort to give specific thanks but consider the impact. Generic gratitude carries less weight. When you are grateful, be precise. Count the good things one by one.

Fenced In

If you are bruised from experiences, sore from sorrow, and you ache from agony in your life, stop giving the pain so much attention. The more attention you give it, the more it will influence your view of the world. What will you magnify? You can take a magnifying glass to your story and select what you are going to make bigger.

Your story can sting.
Your story can soothe.
You choose.

No doubt, people have hurt you. Offenses will come, but that doesn't mean you need to live constantly offended.

I once heard Steven Furtick say that when you take offense, it can start to build a fence between you and others.[13] Don't let your offense become your fence, hemming you in and keeping others out.

I'm not saying ignore the betrayal, lies, pain, accusations, and actions. See them for what they are, arrows you can deflect before they make you bleed. Yes, they will come, because humans hurt humans. But even if the arrow pierces, don't grab it and force it deeper. A protruding arrow will cause you to flinch when you move, and both you and everyone else will see it and suffer.

Instead, grab the arrow that hurt you and pull it out. You will, no doubt, be left wounded, but it will eventually heal. You may never be the same again, but it will not be as bad as leaving the arrow in place, forever hindering your movement and limiting your ability to pass through small places and press on. Don't let the arrow hurt those who dare approach, either. Remove it, creating a clear space for others to get close to you.

Students and Prudent

We got married the year we graduated and had teaching jobs starting in September. We lived that summer on a loan because our first salaries weren't due until the end of our first month of working. Even though we were well educated and had good jobs lined up, it would take a while to recover from student life and claw our way out of debt.

We rented our first house for only six months because the owners decided to sell. They offered it to us first, and in retrospect, we probably should have tried harder to get a mortgage to buy it, because it was in an amazing location and is now worth a fortune. We were served notice having only lived there for four months and needed to find somewhere else, fast.

We hurriedly rented an apartment that was part of a garage in an 18th-century manor house. The gardens of the house were elegantly manicured, and we had stunning views afforded to us by the adjacent orchard. It was beautiful, though exceptionally cold because the very old windows didn't shut properly. It was extremely drafty, and the money we invested into our oil heating just sailed unapologetically into the English countryside, hardly brushing past to warm us on its way out! In the end, we decided we could no longer afford the heating, so our evenings were spent sitting with a little electric heater, under sleeping bags and blankets in our lounge. When it was time for bed, we'd move the heater to the bedroom to warm it up before we needed to get changed. Our bed had two duvets and additional blankets. We slept fully clothed, wearing bobble hats and socks! When we woke, we could see our breath in the cold air, and we had to muster up the courage to step outside the cocoon of our duvet and face the frosty walk to the bathroom.

We stayed in that apartment for eighteen months until we bought our first home. Being handed the keys to our Victorian house in Kent was one of the best days of my life. The house was by no means perfect. For starters, there was an eclipse every time a lorry went past the window, as we were about three feet away from a busy main road. There were no balustrades on the landing, and we could jump over the staircase from one side to the other without having to turn the corner. It was certainly a "project," and neither Nik nor I are DIY people at all! We absolutely loved that house. It was ours and it was warm. We didn't own much furniture and didn't mind one bit. Our sofas were my parents' old ones, and since I grew up in a house where hospitality was a major theme, they were showing the strain of having hosted thousands of bottoms over the years. We happily used secondhand furniture instead of buying new, and invested our money into travel and adventure instead.

What I Saw at the Sawmill

We recently commissioned a dining table to be made from a two-hundred-year-old oak tree felled in Thetford Forest, England. The carpenter worked with this beautiful wood to create a piece of furniture we'd waited many years for. This may seem unspectacular to you, and rightly so. But to us, it is a big deal. This is the first dining table we've ever bought, and we don't foresee getting another one anytime soon.

On our visit to the sawmill, we looked as out of place as a someone wearing ski gear on a beach in the height of summer. We arrived directly from work, and Nik was wearing his suit and brogues. I was in my posh boots, and our son was in his school uniform, traipsing through mud and slush. We looked comical as we tottered among slabs of aged timber. It was fascinating. I love listening to experts talking passionately about their area of skill. In this instance, trees. We watched as the sawmill staff choreographed the trees around the yard. Eager to share more, they took us to the back of the site and talked us through the machinery and wood they had worked on that day.

It was here I saw a tree trunk cut into round pieces, a little like a stack of discs, one on top of the other. At the top I could see a dark gray patch in the wood, about halfway between the perimeter and the center of it. The expert explained that someone had hit two nails into the tree. Looking at the age of the tree and the location of the nails, he guessed it had happened maybe thirty years before. The tree had continued to grow around the nails and bury them deep into its trunk. On first appearance, no one would have known the nails were there. In fact, had he sawed just a few millimeters higher, he wouldn't have known, either. Unfortunately for him, though, he had snagged the blade of his saw as he cut through the trunk. Those two nails stopped him in his tracks and caused serious damage. The tree had continued to grow around the nails but was forever compromised. Years later, he started to cut into the tree to find that there was an obstruction, a foreign object embedded where it shouldn't have been. It was ugly, out of place, and probably took quite a bit of force to be pushed in there in the first place. Those nails damaged the tree then and continued to cause damage thirty years later.

It occurs to me that this is a little like offense. When someone bangs a nail or two into your "bark," either maliciously or unintentionally, what do you do? Notice the question here. I am not asking: "Have you ever been offended?" The question is: "What do you do when you are offended?" Do you bury it deep, or do you yank it out? Is it still causing pain, or have you removed it as far from yourself as you can, minimizing the damage as much as possible?

If someone threw you a grenade with the pin pulled, would you put it in your pocket or throw it far from you? I wonder if we're tempted to put offense in our pocket. We carry it around with us and allow the damage to continue day after day, year after year. We take it out, revisit it, re-examine it, remind the person who upset us and everyone else about it, and put it back in our pocket again for a later date. Maybe for the next time that person hurts us or in case someone else says or does something similar. If we are not careful, we can start to accrue an entire arsenal of offenses that are damaging, limiting, and toxic to ourselves and those in our world.

I often ask myself "What Does It Matter?" to move on, forgive, and throw the grenade as far from me as possible. When I ask myself that question, it requires me to assess the magnitude of the offense. I remind myself I can decide the extent to which I will allow this to matter to my life, or not. What at first may seem like a big deal can be put into perspective pretty quickly if we ask "What Does It Matter?" with an honest and open mind.

How about when you are the one throwing the grenades? I know I hurt people sometimes. We all do. When apologizing, do you take the grenade back and put it in your backpack to cause you damage forever? Can you forgive yourself? Or do you sincerely apologize and then throw the grenade to the horizon, where it can't hurt either of you anymore?

Our ability for metacognition means we can think about what we are thinking about. This can help to put us in control. If a close friend of yours did something wrong and felt truly sorry for their behavior, what would you say to them? Would you be gracious towards them? Would you respond to their humility with harsh words or with compassion? Do you ever step back in the moment, recognize what you are feeling, and treat yourself with the same kindness you would treat a friend?

It is helpful, I find, to see the offense as separate from the offender. It is a decision or an action that has provoked a certain response. The hurt is not a human. It is the result of someone's behavior and seeing it as such helps us to process it. The object of the offense needs to be addressed as separately from the individual as possible. Try to separate the act or attitude from the person. Is the person "bad," or did they make a bad or thoughtless decision?

Your Right to Be Right

If you choose to dwell on the negative, you may be justified but miserable. Emancipation awaits those who are willing to abandon their right to be right. Is it possible to leave it behind in its squalor of bitterness and step onto the peaceful road to freedom?

> How would your life change if you decided to forgive?

Is being "the one in the right" worth the heartache?

> "Forgiveness liberates the soul. It removes fear.
> That is why it is such a powerful weapon."
> —Nelson Mandela[14]

There is no doubt offense will come. Bad situations will happen. Pain will punctuate our life. I've had my fair share of reasons to hold a grudge, but to what consequence? Who am I hurting? Holding a grudge is akin to taking a grenade someone else has thrown at me and popping it in my pocket. I may even zip it up to keep it safe and then put a big ugly sign on that pocket, just so everyone else knows I'm offended, why, and by whom. It is in my power to recognize it for what it is and throw it as far away from me and my loved ones as possible, reducing its impact and power to cause damage.

To Do or Not to Do

We hold forgiveness. It is in our possession and under our charge. It is in our control to release it. We are not expected to go on the hunt for some treasure outside of ourselves to be able to forgive; it requires us to look at what is already in our hands and to choose to give it.

Unforgiveness is appealing in part because it is seemingly so justifiable. It can even look honorable not to forgive. Other damaging behaviors are more proactive. They can be seen and avoided in advance. To have an affair is a "to do, or not to do" kind of thing. An affair is always damaging to at least one party. A decision to act like that can be overcome in the moment by leaving a room, ceasing communication, relocating, changing jobs, willpower—whatever it takes. It is a conscious act.

Unforgiveness is different because it is present whether we like it or not. We start there until we choose to forgive. This is very different from unfaithfulness, lying, or theft, for example, where you start from a good place and choose the bad. With forgiveness, you are in a bad place until you choose the good.

The allure of not forgiving is very real, unseen, and undramatic. It resides in secret and is seemingly innocuous. You aren't doing any harm to anyone by not forgiving, are you? You're not actively choosing to be spiteful. You are the victim, you are the one who is hurt. It is your right to be offended, right?

Unforgiveness is more difficult to detect than some other toxic thinking because it is stealthily hidden and creeps up oh so quietly, allowing bitterness and unease to take root and grow. It is a wolf in sheep's clothing because, at first glance, it is easy to justify and even applaud, but it leads to destruction and ugliness. Sometimes we don't decide to withhold forgiveness, it's just that we didn't make a decision to release it. Bitterness can fester, suffocating ourselves and others around us in a repulsive fog that reeks of ruin.

The longer you nurture your wound, the larger it grows. In fact, whatever you nurture grows. If you nurture bitterness, if you tend it, defend it, and feed it, it will grow. If you nurture self-pity, explain it, justify it, and cater to it, it will grow. If you nurture joy, look for it, express it, celebrate it, and share it, it will grow.

Perhaps someone threw a punch, but you nourished that bruise until it grew into something so big it could have been created by a torpedo. Things can escalate out of all proportion, causing both seen and unseen damage.

Could this invitation to forgive be an invitation to freedom? I'm not talking about the freedom of the person who wounded you. I'm talking about your freedom. It is an invitation to live a happier life with better, healthier relationships. What do you feel stirring inside of you as you read this?

For the Victim and the Offended

The decision to forgive others is not just for the sake of those who hurt and offended us. It is also for us, the hurt and offended. We hold forgiveness in ourselves and have the power to give it to someone else.

Eva Kor was taken to Auschwitz concentration camp in May 1944. Together with her twin sister, Miriam, she was used for human experimentation by Dr. Mengele and his team, undergoing months of torture. The ten-year-old girls were subjected to humiliating, traumatic, and physically harmful procedures which Eva says put the children "through hell." The two sisters lost their entire family. The last time they saw their mother, she was distressed and calling out for her children, arms outstretched as they were separated and taken in two different directions. One to the gas chambers and one to "work," which meant for the twins, being the subjects of human experimentation.

Having survived Auschwitz, Eva moved from Romania to Israel to serve in the Israeli army before getting married and becoming a US citizen. On May 6, 1986, at a ceremony to remember the Holocaust, Kor was heard screaming as she was dragged away by US Capitol police:

"...a bystander on the periphery of the Rotunda who began shouting and waving a placard, disrupting Wiesel's speech—recalled the Nazi past. When asked to put her sign down, she threw herself to the floor and was dragged, screaming, out of the room by two U.S. Capitol Police officers, her screams echoing down the hallway. 'I do not know what it is,' Wiesel said at the podium after she was escorted out, 'but

I am pained whenever I hear anyone cry. I am pained whenever I hear anyone shout.' The woman, later identified as Eva Kor, 52, of Terre Haute, Ind., was initially arrested for disorderly conduct, then released without charges, according to U.S. Capitol Police Inspector Bob Howe. Kor's placard, according to police, read: 'Memorial ceremonies are not enough. We want open hearings on Mengele-gate. I am on a hunger strike.'"[15]

She demanded justice, and rightly so. But then, nearly fifty years after her release from the death camp, she spoke publicly about forgiveness and how it changed her life. She says she felt an enormous weight lifted from her.

"I knew that was a crazy idea, to thank a Nazi—a survivor of Auschwitz to thank a Nazi. People would think that I have lost my mind. I tried to figure out how to thank him and after 10 months, a simple idea popped into my head. How about a letter of forgiveness from me, the survivor of Auschwitz? I knew that that was a meaningful gift for him. But what I discovered for myself was life-changing. That I had the power to forgive. No-one could give me that power. No-one could take it away. To challenge myself, I decided I could even forgive Mengele—the person who had put me through hell. It wasn't easy, but I felt an enormous weight had been lifted from me. I finally felt free. Who decided that I as a victim must be, for the rest of my life, sad, angry, feel hopeless and helpless? I refuse it. You can never change what happened in the past. All you can do is change how you react to it. My sister and I were made into human guinea pigs. Our whole family was murdered. But I have the power to forgive. And so do you."[16]

I have such respect for Eva Kor. She had the strength to forgive the men who had tortured her and murdered her family. I honestly don't know if I could the same, but the fact that she did tells us it is possible. It was hard to forgive them but in doing so, according to Eva, she finally felt free.

There may be genuinely huge issues and events that have overshadowed your life. Forgiving is not easy, and you may need to seek professional help.

With forgiveness, the decision may be transactional (releasing it to someone else), but the process may be transitional (an emotional healing that may happen over time).

● Minor Injuries

Some wounds are minor but can still result in bickering and unrest. For such issues, the answer to "What Does It Matter?" may be far less consequential. It is easier, in this circumstance, to quickly throw the grenade as far away as possible. I need to ask myself "What Does It Matter?" to put those small things into perspective. That golden question puts the brakes on the wheels of something running downhill in my mind, gathering speed and perceived importance as it accelerates out of control.

When irritated, I find it helpful to take a few deep breaths and maybe even go and be by myself, process things, and then come back to the situation. One of the first things to ask in that moment is "What am I angry about?" This sounds obvious, but it's helpful. Identifying exactly why you are angry can help you process your feelings in a healthy way. It is OK to be angry. There are situations where anger is justified and right. Your anger is an emotion. It is data that is telling you something. Notice what you are angry about and why. Allow that information to direct your continued response to the situation or person at hand.

Manage your anger by using the WDIM framework to help guide your thinking.

⬤ WHAT DOES IT MATTER?

What	What am I feeling? Notice and name your feelings.
Define	What, exactly, is the real issue?
Importance/ Impact	Ask yourself "What Does It Matter?" Be honest about how important the issue is to you. Think about the real impact.
Make a Plan	Choose to act or to let it go.

⬤ Manage Your Anger

What: What are you feeling? In this instance, anger.

Define: What, exactly, are you angry about?

Importance: To what extent is the issue important to you or others? Answer this with an open mind. What is the real impact of the offense or situation?

Make a Plan: What needs to happen in order for you to respond appropriately to anger? How can the issue be resolved? Does it need to be resolved, or can you let it go?

Anger may not be the problem. What you say or do in that moment of anger may be. Who do you hurt when you are angry? How do you treat others?

I remember my mom saying "It's OK to be angry. You must choose what you do with that anger, though." She was highlighting that we can use our anger for good or bad. We can turn it in on ourselves (rarely helpful) or throw it at others (also, not always helpful).

Life is too short to carry the burden of other people's mistakes. Too brief to carry the weight of other people's bad decisions and behavior. It is enough to process and manage our own reckless behavior without deciding to be laden down by that of others.

The Discipline to Go Slow

When we think about the grudges we harbor, perhaps we can see the benefit of letting them loose, and letting ourselves loose in the process. I wonder, though, if we fail to notice seeds of bitterness growing. Perhaps we are unaware of our burden of unforgiveness because we haven't taken the time to stop, think, and search our own hearts and minds. Perhaps you are living with an uneasy sense of anger, but you haven't really given yourself time to consider where that stems from. Western culture is living at a fast pace, and we are in danger of replacing reflection and rest with distraction and doing. How do we slow ourselves down enough to process, notice, and choose good thinking?

Being extremely busy all the time may seem productive in the short term, but in the long term, our productivity decreases, our stress increases, and we drive the complex creation of our mind and body into the ground. Our brain needs time to think, to reflect, and to clean. If we forge on ahead without giving our brain the fuel it needs by way of meditation and reflection, we should be unsurprised when we splutter to a standstill at the side of the road. It requires discipline to prioritize time to think, reflect, meditate, and be mindful. These practices are food for our mind, and our mind starts behaving badly when it is hungry for these moments.

A controversial study published in 2014 by researchers from the University of Virginia and Harvard found that "participants typically did not enjoy spending 6 to 15 minutes in a room by themselves with nothing to do but think, that they enjoyed doing mundane external activities much more, and that many preferred to administer electric shocks to themselves instead of being left alone with their thoughts. Most people seem to prefer to be doing something rather than nothing, even if that something is negative."[17]

Yes, according to the study, many people would prefer to give themselves painful electric shocks rather than be left alone with their thoughts for up to fifteen minutes!

Do you relate? Have you lost the skill of being alone with your thoughts? So many people equate thinking time to boredom and/or wasted time. We want to be entertained. We need a sense of purpose and meaning to our lives, and thinking can, on the surface, feel less rewarding. Sitting in a room doing nothing for fifteen minutes can feel aimless. We like to be active and feel we are in control, even if our activity would cause harm. Thinking time can be wrongly construed as wasting time. This stems from the, often subconscious, misconception that thinking is fruitless, unnecessary, and unproductive.

I remember apologizing to my supervisor at Cambridge, because I hadn't done much work one week. I said: "All I did was think about the problem." She answered with a life-changing comment: "Emma, you do realize that thinking is doing?" She encouraged me to understand that thinking was as valuable as doing any other tangible task. It was a eureka moment for me. I now actively allocate thinking time in my day, and I am more productive for it.

● Train Your Brain

Mindfulness, meditation, and prayer are muscles we can develop over time. It is very difficult to go and sit in a room and be alone with your thoughts for fifteen minutes if you have not practiced and developed the stamina to do it.

> "Research has shown that minds are difficult to control, however, and it may be particularly hard to

steer our thoughts in pleasant directions and keep them there. This may be why many people seek to gain better control of their thoughts with meditation and other techniques, with clear benefits. Without such training, people prefer doing to thinking, even if what they are doing is so unpleasant that they would normally pay to avoid it. The untutored mind does not like to be alone with itself."

"Just Think: The Challenges of the Disengaged Mind"[18]

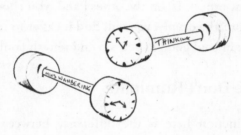

Imagine running a marathon with no training. You'd struggle and potentially be furious at yourself for failing. You might even think that running is not for you, you just weren't cut out for it, and that watching TV from a sofa suits you far better. Your failure may lead you to give up, but failure to run your marathon was likely because there was no habit, no strength, and no incremental advancement.

If you are out of the practice of running, don't start with a marathon! Begin with intermittent walking and short bursts of running. Build up stamina and increase your fitness over time until you can keep running for longer.

This is a little like meditation or thinking time. Your level of concentration may only be in short bursts to start with and that's OK. You need to start where you are and build up the mental fitness to sit alone with your thoughts for longer periods. It takes a different kind of strength to slow yourself down, breathe deeply, and give your brain a break. Don't be hard on yourself if your concentration is limited to begin with. Start with small moments and build it up incrementally.

Mindfulness will help you cope better with anxiety and stress. It may even help you avoid them in the first place. Your brain needs to be fit and clear. Help it by training it. Discipline your thinking. Build that muscle up little by little. Learn to like your thoughts and not see being alone with them as being behind enemy lines. Use your thinking to your benefit and not your downfall.

Let's go back to the two rivers metaphor for a moment. You are more likely to drink stinking thinking if you are running fast and competitively against others. If, on the other hand, you choose to pause, sit at a table, and breathe deeply, you will find it easier to reach for healthy water and do your soul good as you sip and refresh your mind.

● Meditate Don't Ruminate

A helpful distinction here is the difference between self-reflection, which is good, and rumination, which is not always good for us. Amy Morin, author of *13 Things Mentally Strong People Don't Do*, says that dwelling on negative events and distressing emotions isn't good for a number of reasons.[19] It can lead to mental health problems and may mean those mental health problems last longer. She says it is a hard cycle to break, and it can, not always, but sometimes, increase the risk of falling into unhealthy coping mechanisms such as substance abuse and eating disorders. So, what does she suggest we do to help ourselves stop ruminating (or stop drinking stinking thinking) to our own detriment?

1. Recognize when it's happening.
2. Look for solutions. (Don't just think about the problem. Think about solutions to that problem.)

3. Set aside time to think. Plan thinking time in your day and only allow yourself to think about that problem then, within a tight timeframe.
4. Distract yourself. Moving around is helpful. Don't try to simply not think about something. Rather, replace it with something else instead.
5. Practice mindfulness.[20]

Ethan Kross, Professor of Psychology and Management/Organizations at the University of Michigan and the author of *Chatter*, has conducted research around our "internal voice" and how we may be able to reroute our internal dialogues to make them work for us rather than against us. He uses the term "chatter" to describe the cycle of negative thoughts and feelings we experience when our minds are getting away from us.[21] Negative chatter can adversely affect key areas of our life, including our thinking and performance, our relationships, and our physical and mental well-being.

Ruminating is focusing on one thing over and over. When our attention is focused on one thing, it is not given to something else, including the ones we love. It can adversely affect our relationships and even push people away. To gain support we, quite rightly, talk to others about our problems. But our relationships can get damaged when we keep talking about the same issues over and over again, because it can be draining for other people. Kross says this talking over the same problem can act as a social repellent, pushing others away. His research shows that while it is good to talk about our feelings because we want people to validate them and we need to feel supported, there are also downsides to oversharing. We run the danger of what Kross calls "co-rumination."[22] This is where we may receive validation, but the chatter doesn't end. The cycle continues, just with someone else joining in!

So, what is the answer? First, find someone to talk to who can validate how you are feeling, ensuring you feel loved and understood. This part of a healthy conversation may last for different lengths of time depending on the circumstances, personality, and needs of people involved. For some it may be thirty seconds, thirty minutes, or several hours. Second, the conversation needs to move on so you can find solutions and reframe things. This balance of both emotional support and reasoned thinking can help people break free of a rumination cycle. In short, don't just talk it over, also look for solutions. Rumination can damage our physical and mental well-being. Chatter can cause our stress levels to rise and have a profound physiological impact on our health. Stress in the right context and the right amount is healthy. Our emotions give us information, and we should listen to their signaling and act. The problem comes when our stress response is triggered and remains high. When we ruminate, we may simulate a threat unnecessarily, raising our stress response, which affects our sleeping, eating, and ability to function.

Breaking the cycle of internal chatter and negative thinking is a powerful skill to learn. It is simple to implement and can have a deep and meaningful impact on our lives. So, how does Kross suggest we break the cycle?

1. **Use your name when addressing yourself in thinking.** Distancing is helpful because we are better at giving other people advice than we are at giving it to ourselves. When we use our own name, we distance ourselves from the problem and give ourselves much more objective feedback. We trick our brain into giving the advice it may have given a friend in the same situation, which is often better than the advice we may have thought to give ourselves.

2. **Harness relationships with other people.** As already discussed, this is most helpful when it is with people who can both validate your feelings and help you to break free from the chatter cycle by helping you find solutions. Let's also make an effort to help our friends by implementing this two-step process. The next

time someone talks to you about their problems, first help them by validating their feelings. Second, help them find a solution.

3. **Interact with our physical environments.** When we get a sense of awe and wonder from the world around us, it helps to put our problems into perspective. Science shows that awe is a powerful way to broaden our perspective. We perceive our own concerns relative to the things around us, and they can seem a lot smaller than they once did. Psychologists call this the "shrinking of self" and, in this instance, if that means shrinking your problems, that's a good thing.[23]

Your thinking directly influences your feelings, and your feelings influence your choices. If you learn to use your thinking to your advantage rather than disadvantage, it will enhance your physical and mental well-being and will benefit the people around you. When you capture your thoughts and make them work for you, you can find freedom in forgiving others, break negative thinking cycles, and choose to focus your thoughts on the good.

Two rivers to drink from. On the mountain in Russia, my life depended on getting it right. When it comes to your life, what thinking are you drinking? Your life really does depend on it.

What Does It Matter?...
...What I Expect?

GREAT EXPECTATIONS

● Trinkets and Treasure

On an October day in Central Park, New York, an old gentleman carefully laid out his art. He was wearing a white baseball cap, sunglasses, blue shirt, knitted vest, and a money bag tied around his waist. His stall was pitched next to others selling tourist memorabilia, trinkets, and snacks. He painstakingly placed each piece of art, ensuring each could be fully seen and none were damaged. Some were on the trestle table or hung using cable ties on the wired backdrop. A few were on the floor, propped up against the table legs waiting their turn for prominence. Paintings that were hung to one side had the sunlight shining through them, while those opposite were shaded by a white umbrella. Three canvases took center stage. In the middle, a sign sprayed in black on a white landscape canvas said: "SPRAY ART." To its right sat another white canvas with a black circular shape in the middle with "$60" stenciled on it. And to the left was another black canvas stating, "This is not a photo opportunity" sprayed in white. Satisfied with his display, the old gentleman sat down in his folding chair next to his stall and quietly waited.

At 11 a.m. he opened the stall. People chatted as they passed by, and their conversations arrived into his soundtrack of the hustle and bustle of New York, then faded into the cacophony of the city again as they carried on past him and out of sight. He would hear snippets of conversations, some more than others, depending on their walking pace. A horse-drawn carriage passed behind the stall, driven by a man wearing a top hat and featuring the American flag floating in a breeze carrying the temptation of hot dogs. The carriage riders were unable to see the artwork clearly and were seemingly unfussed, quickly turning their attention elsewhere. At 12:30 p.m. the old gentleman was seen yawning while a sightseeing bus drove by, packed with tourists searching for the spectacular. At 1:30 p.m. he had yet to make a single sale. He ate his lunch, undisturbed, next to his stall.

At 3:30 p.m. the old gentleman got his first sale. A lady bought two canvases as gifts for her grandchildren. She negotiated him down 50 percent, buying two for the price of one, and placed the canvases, along with her other shopping, in a transparent blue carrier bag. He smiled at his first sale, four hours after opening. At 4 p.m. Arnika Juvalta from New Zealand bought another two, and the gentleman shook her hand and kissed her goodbye. He was delighted as much as she was by her purchase. At 5:30 p.m. a man from Chicago said, "I just need something for the walls," and he bought four. He, too, got a hug from the old gentleman, and he smiled as he carried away two small canvases in a blue bag and two larger ones under his arm. At 6 p.m. the gentleman stood, clippers in hand, to take down the unsold art. His total takings for the day were $420. He packed the remaining canvases and table and swiftly left the park.

This gentleman's day would have been unremarkable had it not been for the fact that the paintings for sale were originals by the famous British artist, Banksy. The following day Banksy put a message out on his website explaining his work had been for sale. He stated this was a one-time-only thing, and he would not be doing it again.

In 2019, Banksy's painting "Devolved Parliament" sold for a record £8.5 million at Sotheby's in London. Had those exact paintings from Central Park been on sale in an art gallery with the artist's name written clearly on them, they would have sold for over a thousand times the value. How do I know? Well, Arnika Juvalta went on to sell her two prints for $200,000.

Can you imagine how many people walked past the investment of a lifetime? An amazing opportunity totally overlooked by so many. How did it happen?

People walking along Central Park that day did not expect to see a Banksy original selling for so little in such an ordinary place. And because they didn't expect it, they didn't see it. Their expectations acted as a lens.

Have we missed significant things in our lives because we were not looking for them? Have we misunderstood, misinterpreted, and mistaken anything to be what it was not? Is there treasure in your everyday ordinary life that is going unnoticed? Are you expecting the "perfect life"? I remember watching one weather forecast that said residents going through a flood warning were "...hoping for the best but expecting the worst." What do you hope for? What are you expecting? Are they the same?

> Our expectations significantly affect our experience.

Outlook and Outcome

Imagine this: Two men working away in a field. Both were picking the same amount of cotton, working with the same tools, and working at the same pace. Both needed to pick the same volume of cotton before their work was done. One man was working with fervor and a smile on his face. He exuded joy with every backbreaking bend of his body. The other worked hard but without the same level of enthusiasm.[24]

What affected the different attitudes of these two men? One was told they would be paid one hundred pounds for the day's work and the other £1 million. Their expectation of the reward was so vastly different, it dramatically affected their experience of the job. To one, the one hundred pounds seemed fair and worth the work, but nothing to get all excited about. The other, clearly, could not believe it would take so little to earn so much. This meant his work seemed less arduous because the experience differed in light of the reward. Expectation of reward naturally affected their experience of the work.

Our expectation of life dramatically influences our experience. Expecting luxury and experiencing less than average somehow feels much worse than expecting poor quality and having those low expectations met. Fake standards set by social media and entertainment can feel out of reach, especially when we discover the fiction we've been feeding our minds is not aligned with reality.

Do you feel a constant and ongoing pressure to make your life "picture perfect"? Our hope for perfect inflates our expectations of what life should be, leaving us disappointed when our own expectations aren't met. When striving for perfect, it is all too easy to heap unnecessary demands upon an already crowded day.

Have you ever caught yourself remarking that you are finding it hard to juggle everything, and therefore you don't feel like you are doing anything particularly well? Nothing seems quite good enough, and you shoulder this quiet burden that whispers: "You're a failure."

Are you really failing, or is it that your expectation was unrealistic in the first place? Is it possible that to have managed what you already have is amazing? It is no surprise that you feel like you are failing if the standard you are setting yourself is unattainable. If your to-do list is beyond doable, don't be surprised when you struggle to do it.

The Shame Train

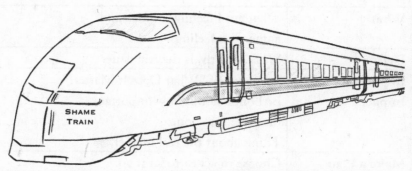

EXPECTATION EXPRESS

Can you remember a time when:

1. You set extremely high (unrealistic) expectations of what you might achieve.
2. You then ran yourself ragged trying to achieve what was unachievable.
3. You then felt cross with yourself for not achieving it.
4. You were hard on yourself, saying things over in your head like: "I'm a failure," or, "Why can't I manage everything better?" or "I'm just not coping."
5. You felt shame and/or guilt for falling short of what you expected you could achieve.
6. You went to bed weary, woke up the next morning, and started at number 1 again.

Yeah, me neither! How can we break this cycle? The answer lies in number 1. Let's set better expectations in the first place! We need to give ourselves a fighting chance of going to bed satisfied with our day.

Wouldn't that feel marvelous? To go to bed satisfied with our day...

WDIM: If you have realistic expectations on what you can achieve?

What	What am I feeling? Notice and name your feelings.
Define	What, exactly, is the real issue?
Importance/ Impact	Ask yourself "What Does It Matter?" Be honest about how important the issue is to you. Think about the real impact.
Make a Plan	Choose to act or to let it go.

Manage Your Expectations

What: Feeling overwhelmed that things aren't perfect and are left incomplete.

Define: I need to feel more in control and less like I'm failing. Something needs to give. I'd rather choose to "put down" than "drop."

Importance/Impact: I need to take action because feeling I'm constantly failing is horrible. I want to break the cycle. I need to de-escalate the situation and assess things one by one. Even the process of choosing priorities is helpful, as it reminds me that not everything is equal and not everything matters as much as other things.

Make a Plan: Anything that does not fit in my "five to thrive" list is potentially going to get put down. Everything in my "five to thrive" stays.

● Five to Thrive

The "five to thrive" advice my mom gave me fights for my sanity when I feel I'm not doing anything well. You've probably heard of the "fruit and veg five-a-day" nutritional advice. This is my "five-a-day" list, and I use it frequently.

I regularly ask myself, is everyone:

1. Safe?
2. Fed?
3. Clean?
4. Warm?
5. Loved?

If the answer is no to any of those and it is within your ability to act, do so and do so swiftly. If it is not in your ability to fulfil this checklist for whatever reason, then please reach out for help.

If your answer to all these questions is yes, then relax. Those things being in place is your treasure, right there. When you feel battered and rocked by the storm of everyday life, find relief in the harbor of your five to thrive.

● Give Yourself a Break

Humanity has survived for centuries with that five-to-thrive checklist working just fine. Don't be tempted to add "with the best stroller money can buy, the latest shoes, the perfectly decorated house, the most exquisite library of children's books (all in alphabetical order and within easy reach of the bed), the perfect outfit with no mess, all homework completed to a gold standard, high-income work, house tidy, and picture-perfect life for social media." You are going to wear yourself out if you do, because you are aiming at something that is exhausting to reach, and if on the rare occasion you do reach it, is almost impossible to maintain. Do you ever have one room tidy and clean only to look behind you and find your children have been "creative" in another space?

Sidenote—it seems to be impossible to encourage creativity and lessen screen time with our kids while also maintaining a perfectly clean and tidy house. Give yourself a break! You can choose to look at the camp in the living room, the Legos in the dining room, the arts and crafts in the kitchen, and the dress up clothes all over the bedroom floor and berate yourself for not having a tidy home. Or you can celebrate that your kids are being creative, learning, and having fun. Your choice. Creativity and fun can result in a hurricane of mess. A messy house is part of the process of nurturing your child's creativity and adventure. How can you nurture a child's curiosity while scolding them for rummaging through a drawer investigating your Tupperware? They are adventurers of their little world. To us it's a messy kitchen. To them it's learning, inspiration, independence, motor skills, and fun! Of course, it can be annoying. But take a deep breath. Let them explore, then ask them to help you put it all back again once their little adventure is over. They won't see re-stacking and tidying up as the chore we do, they'll enjoy it! Get them involved in the tidy up.

Curiosity and creative play are key to bringing up young adults who are problem solvers and solution finders. If we place our adult boundaries and need for clean on our children all the time, we could restrict their freedom and feed their anxiety.

When Rest Is Best

"What Does It Matter?" if your living room is a mess? Truth is, sometimes it does, sometimes it doesn't. The trick is knowing when it matters and when it doesn't. The answer cannot be the same at all times.

To take pride in our homes is a good thing, but let's not let desire for perfection drive us to misery.

Don't let organizing the trinkets cause you to overlook the treasure.

Go back to basics. Is everyone OK? Are our basic needs being met? Almost everything else is peripheral. Don't get me wrong, I like to have a tidy house. I love it when work is enjoyable and fulfilling, my clothes are ironed, and my house admin is up to date. But if I use these things as a measure of whether I am succeeding or not, I will be on a roller coaster of failure one minute and success the next. Celebrate those days when you've got it all together. Just be kinder to yourself when you don't. If everyone is safe, fed, clean, warm, and loved, you're doing fine.

When under pressure, I can find it difficult to articulate what exactly is pressing too hard on me. Asking myself that list of questions helps to uncover what is bothering me. When using my "five to thrive," the source of my anxiety becomes clear and subsequently conquered. If my anxiety levels start to rise as I feel the horizon of my children's hunger getting closer, I name it, make a plan for it, and relax.

If the cause of my stress does not sit within the "five-to-thrive" list, it is likely that it isn't as big a deal as I think. Set expectations of yourself that allow you to thrive and, dare I say it, enjoy everyday life a little more.

> Find treasure in the ordinary and unexpected places. It is there, if only you'd perceive it.

● Love Me, Love Me

The desire to be accepted is strutting its neediness on social media every day. It is natural to want the approval of others, but at what cost? I perceive it as a growing value in today's culture.

Do you spend money you don't have, to impress people you've never met? Do you change your viewpoint to please those around you? Are you easily led? Do you require others' approval to the extent you become afraid and unwilling to fail? If you are afraid to fail, you are less likely to try new things and less likely to grow.

Growth Mindset

Dr. Carol Dweck and her colleagues at Stanford University have identified what they call a "growth mindset."[25] I see the results of their research to be true in my own life.

During my teenage years, I was on a scholarship to a local music school. I was told I was a good pianist and I lived trying to prove everyone right. What if it turned out I wasn't a brilliant pianist after all? I never wanted to make mistakes, so I made sure that I practiced in private. Every time I did make mistakes publicly, they had a disproportionate impact on me. This fear of making a mistake eventually led to the stunting of my growth as a musician and halted my journey to excellence. I settled for distinctly average, at best! I never discovered how good I could become because I was embarrassed to get things wrong in front of people.

In the first week of University, I turned up to a big band rehearsal with my trumpet only to find that there were lots of other brass players there, most of whom were better than me. The brass section was full, but the piano stool was empty. The band leader asked the nervous row of freshers if any of us played the piano. I said I did and that was that. My first study was classical piano, but I was thrust into a situation where I had to play in a very different style. I needed to play jazz. I played a lot by ear and knew how to read a chord chart, so I managed to start and finish with everyone else, and it turned out that was good enough. I was given the seat of pianist for the jazz band.

I was fine at vamping (just playing along with everyone else), but every single time it was my turn for a solo, I looked up with "help me" eyes at the band leader and simply refused. Shaking my head, I would say out loud, "Nope." Even in a rehearsal situation I couldn't bring myself to look foolish. I wanted everyone to think I was a good pianist. Of course, I just showed myself to be the insecure and limited musician I was, and I missed out on a fantastic opportunity to grow. I was the only girl in the band, too, and I wanted to look like I could keep up. It became obvious very quickly that I couldn't. It is one of my few regrets. If someone had just shown me modal playing and given me the confidence to unlock everything, things could have been so different. I played with the band for years and had a great time, but I restricted my progress. I was there to learn, but too embarrassed to admit I didn't know everything.

I was operating with what Dr. Carol Dweck calls a "fixed mindset." I didn't try, I didn't ask for help, I didn't want to seem weak, and in doing so, I became weak. Feeling threatened by failure and mistakes, I ran the other way. This mindset put a glass ceiling on my development as a musician. You make mistakes when you are learning, so by refusing to make mistakes, I, in essence, refused to learn.

That was then. Now I absolutely have a growth mindset! I am consistently brave at giving things a go. My usual answer is: "I don't know, but I can work it out." Or: "No idea, but I may be able to learn." My team roll their eyes when I say these things because they know I genuinely believe them and I will, in fact, go and learn. I can be infuriating to work with because I believe almost anything is possible, and in living out that belief, we find most things are.

I love learning, and I know making errors and finding things difficult is part of that journey. I have finally shaken off my confining panic of failure and embraced the wild landscape of not caring so much what others think of me, so long as I am making progress.

It's Not Me, It's You

One of the hardest lessons I learned early in my working life (I almost wrote career, but I've never actually had one of those!) is that not everyone will accept me.

On one of my first outings as a research assistant I had the privilege of attending a training program for an established UK government department. I politely, introduced myself to people. I held my hand out to initiate the greeting, smiled, told them my name, and asked their names in return. It was simple courtesy. I was shocked and hurt when, in the group discussion that followed, a gentleman informed us he was intimidated by me. He said I shouldn't have been so confident during our introduction because it made him feel small. Apparently, I shouldn't have initiated a hello and asked him how his day was, I should have stood silently to make him feel better about not having the confidence to hold a conversation.

I had simply reached out to be friendly. I was not arrogant, bullish, or overbearing. I know because I asked the lead consultant to tell me the truth.

"Emma, some people will be intimidated by you no matter how you behave because their intimidation is not about you, it is about them."

I still feel ashamed as I recall that moment. I know I didn't do anything wrong, and if in the same situation today, I'd initiate conversation and work to put others at ease. I want to ensure everyone in the room feels comfortable. This is silly and very much part of my "savior complex" because I know it is not my responsibility but, if not mine, then whose? And anyway, in this case, it was my responsibility. I was on the hosting team!

That situation stuck with me because I suspect had I been male, it would have bothered this gentleman less. Had I been a little older and male, it probably would have suited him just fine. I remember being shocked because I approached the introduction with the utmost respect for this man and had no idea, he had so little for himself.

Do you ever feel that you are too much for people? Do you ever feel that you're not enough for others? I find I am either too much for some or not enough for others.

This is partly because we cannot please everybody. This truth is important for us to embrace, so take a deep breath and focus....

Someone accepting you is as much about them as it is about you, and you can only control one part of that equation.

Again.

You could be Dr. Perfect, and there would still be a few who would find you hard to be around because you have it all together. On the other hand, if you don't have it all together, there will be some who find you hard to be around for that reason, too.

> Someone accepting you is as much about them, as it is about you.

You cannot be accepted by everyone.

Everyone will not accept you.

Not everyone will like you.

Be OK with that.

Amazing liberation is yours if you decide you don't need to be liked by everyone.

What Does It Matter?

What Does It Matter if you can't be accepted by everyone?

What Does It Matter if you don't have everyone's approval?

Well, do you like you?

Do you accept you?

If you get to the point of accepting who you are and liking who you are, then you can truly start to accept others. Do you ever feel you aren't enough for yourself? I am often frustrated at my shortcomings and am keenly aware of the unattractive qualities of my behavior and personality. But when we accept ourselves, the need to be accepted by others diminishes.

We are social beings, and we need acceptance. We need to feel a sense of belonging. I'm not suggesting we throw off our need to feel accepted. We all need to be loved. We don't need to be loved by everyone, though. Just a close few.

There is, of course, a difference between being accepted and understood. I can think of people who accept and love me but who do not fully understand me. And that's OK. I don't understand them either!

We all need to be affirmed, but to what extent? How important is other people's approval? All these are important questions. Arguably the most significant question underpinning all of these is: Do we accept ourselves? Wanting the approval of others is instinctive, but is it ever achieved at too great a cost? Allowing our hunger for affirmation to lead us down the road of perfectionism may mean we become afraid and unwilling to fail. If we are afraid to fail, we are less likely to try new things and less likely to grow.

Your need to be accepted is a given.

My question is: How many people do you expect to be accepted by?

● Increased Value

I want approval from my husband. I still want him to think of me as funny, smart, beautiful, gentle, and strong. He did think those things once, so it is partly down to me to ensure I stay the best version of me I can. We all grow and change, and he deserves the best I can give him. He made a promise to be faithful to me until death separates us. I consciously try to make it easy for him to keep that promise. Nevertheless, I am not pleasant all the time, and there are days I am horrible to be around. I don't look my best all the time, either. I don't live an unreal existence where I go to sleep and wake up with my hair and makeup perfectly done every day. Overall, though, I do try to improve on the Emma he made that promise to. I want to make the promise easy to keep and hard to break.

We all change as we grow, but let's grow into even better versions of ourselves for our partners. Let's not allow those aspects that our partners fell in love with diminish over time. Let's make it easy for them to choose us again and again every day, because that's what they do.

Daily life can be fun. You just need to choose to make it so. If we were attractive to our partners once, we can be attractive to them today. If we are going to grow and change, let's be sure it is towards a better version of us, not one where all the fun, attractive, and interesting parts have ebbed away, eroded by the dullness of daily life. Relationships should be a little like committing to an investment and seeing that partnership go up in value, not depreciate over time.

It is important to note that I am not only talking physique here. Too often when thinking about improving ourselves, we think about physical attributes and health. Just look at the multibillion-dollar industry telling us to stay looking young in order to stay attractive. This industry preys on people's self-esteem and is pretty awful, really. Aging should, in fact, be celebrated and admired. It should be valued, because the opposite of growing old is much worse! Instead, a whole industry is based on you spending your money to fix something that is not broken. Your body will age. You've been aging since the day you were born, but when you hit forty years old, you're told whatever you do, don't age. And then we wonder why the older generation doesn't get the respect they deserve. Media and consumerism are pushing an "age is bad" message at every corner. I personally think this is a malady of society, and possibly something I should write another book about.

Anyway, on with protecting and growing our investment in our relationships. What about conversation, hobbies, interests, learning, and mindset, among other things? If I "let myself go" will I:

1. Love myself?
2. Be pleasant to be around because I am finding it hard to love myself?
3. Love my partner the best I can by being the best I can for them?

It can feel like a tricky circle because when we are not feeling good about ourselves for whatever reason, we really don't want to up our game and look after ourselves. I get that. It takes disciplining our minds to choose to do the right thing, because doing the wrong thing just makes things worse.

"What Does It Matter?" if we look after ourselves? If we look after our physical, mental, and emotional well-being? Well, partly it helps us to enjoy life. Being grateful is a great way to help look after our thinking. It may take effort, but it will eventually lead us to smile. To enjoy the moment. To reflect on the good. To pause in wonder. To be present. To stop striving. Mindfulness may help you feel calm and happy. That's worth doing, isn't it? Or do you enjoy your misery so much that you are not prepared to be happy? Do you identify yourself with pain and fear what would remain if it left you?

Comfortable Complaining

I think of it a little like swaddling a baby.

Swaddling makes a baby feel cozy and comfortable. A tightly wrapped blanket cocooning the baby brings security and warmth, and allows the baby to feel safe, resting in a soft boundary from which they cannot break free. Some adults like to swaddle in their duvets for the same reason. It feels good!

But what if that blanket was moldy, filthy, and infested with mites? What if it still gives you that sense of security because you know how to operate in that blanket? You know where the boundaries are, you feel weirdly safe, and sleep well. You garner attention and sympathy from those around you. You restrict your movements and stay living a small life. It gives you a reason to take and receive way more than give. What if all those comforting things are true, but your blanket is actually smelly, ugly, and hard to hold? Your hands are tied, right? It gives you a reason to stay still and not grow. You are wrapped and unable to move, right? It draws attention to you, and that feels good, right? It's not your fault, right?

Are you wearing your misery like a comfort blanket? Is that blanket really doing you and others around you good? If circumstances out of your control weaved that blanket of pain and wrapped you up good and tight leaving you weeping, you can still work on removing it.

Your circumstances may have changed, never to be the same again. But you can choose whether you will live in a blanket of bitterness or slowly, gradually, carefully, unwrap yourself and feel the fresh air on your skin. Feel the warmth of the sun again and free your hands to be useful to others. Move without restriction and open yourself up to the world once more.

It is a process, and you may need professional help, but I believe it is doable. I am not diminishing your personal circumstance. I don't even know your personal circumstance. I do know what it is to cry my way through the night, though. To wake up with a heaviness on my chest that makes me feel like I am suffocated by sorrow.

Sadness is a valid and necessary emotion.

On one occasion, I needed to sob so hard and loud there was nowhere in my house private enough not to be heard. So, I put my trainers on, rushed out of the front door, and ran. As I ran, tears streamed down my face until I was sobbing gut-wrenching groans. I roared and allowed the mess of my face to be what it was, a mess. I cried and cried and could hardly catch my breath, all while running through the woods. That way, no one heard, and I could choose to feel my emotions, name my emotions, and allow them to pass through me in private. By the time I got home, I had finished sobbing. I was still sad when I thought about the cause of my pain, but once I was through the ripping emotion, I could choose to focus on something else. Once calm, I turned my mind to learning and distraction.

The issue was not immediately resolved, but I took some time to allow my sadness, grief, and anger to do its work. I took time to allow myself (albeit privately) to sob. My sadness was so intense it forced me to assess my thinking. I am ashamed to admit there was self-pity in the mix, but I needed to hear myself think those thoughts to capture them, name them, and choose not to be like that. I had the chance to ask myself whether my thoughts were true. I literally asked myself whether what I was thinking, and whether this image I had created, this story I was telling myself, was true.

It was true in part. Truth and fact were evident in the story I was telling myself. But I could also focus my attention on a different part of the same story and feel differently. I named the parts that were accurate and called out the overgeneralization and catastrophizing elements.

These were the parts I had exaggerated to placate my own ego and emotions. This saved me from projecting that sadness on someone else or saying something I would later regret.

Go to the TMO

Think of an incident unfolding in front of your eyes with many cameras filming at once. There are facts. Things that are actually happening and cannot be denied. They can though, seem to take a different meaning depending on which camera you are looking through. If you can imagine ten cameras all filming the same thing from different locations, heights, lighting, viewpoints, and perspectives, you can imagine the same scene seen from different angles. The same facts seen from different positions can produce different insights.

When officiating a rugby match, there are times when the referee needs to go to the Television Match Official (TMO).[26] For example, to decide whether a try has been scored. The referee asks the TMO to examine several different angles and camera shots, because looking solely from one position does not give the full picture. Seeing only one viewpoint can lead to a bad decision. It takes an overview of several different angles, including the referee on the pitch, to decipher what actually happened. The one play will look different to the players, the coach on the sidelines, the referee, the spectators, and the TV cameras.

Same facts but differing viewpoints can lead to different interpretations. If you choose to look at your situation through only one lens, you may miss the whole truth. What you see may be factual, but may not be the entire picture. Only when stepping back and viewing the big picture are we able to perceive the full story.

"What Does It Matter?" if you allow yourself to get caught up in your own viewpoint and fail to see things from different angles? It matters because you might end up making a bad decision. It matters because you may think things are worse than they are and you may project your hurt and disappointment onto someone who is not to blame. You may wallow in a pool of sadness which, though valid, is not the whole picture.

Truth matters because it means we are acting on reliable information, and we can respond in an appropriate and helpful way. We may think all is well and we are making good choices. But when we look at the situation from another camera angle, perhaps from the angle of someone else, we may see we need to make a different decision or act differently. Consciously making an effort to see things from other camera angles helps us to see more of the whole picture, and in doing so, will ultimately equip us to make better decisions.

Everything wasn't all solved on that run, but I allowed myself the time and space to journey with my sadness, to get the best out of it. It showed me what I was thinking and doing, and pointed me towards what needed to change. It allowed me the time to reflect and see if there were other angles I could use. I needed to help myself move out of my state of self-pity and into a state of strength. My sadness was justified, but I didn't want to stay there. I needed to move through it.

My question is not whether you will suffer or whether you will feel anxious, sad, fearful, angry, and upset. We all find ourselves in those valleys at times. My question is "What Does It Matter?" when you do? How can you use those uncomfortable emotions to your benefit?

● Helpful Discomfort

Dr. Joan Rosenberg believes there is a gifted wisdom in unpleasant feelings.[27] Notice she makes a point to say that they are not necessarily bad or negative feelings. They are simply uncomfortable and unpleasant. She mentions eight specific feelings she believes are necessary for us to experience and move through. These are sadness, shame, helplessness, anger, vulnerability, embarrassment, disappointment, and frustration. Dr. Rosenberg says that if we manage to stay fully present and aware of these feelings and not avoid them, it will dramatically impact our experience of feeling capable in the world.

When an emotional feeling gets triggered, chemicals are released and then flushed through our system. We feel our emotions as a physical sensation. Our bodies let us know what we are feeling. According to Dr. Rosenberg, this chemical rush lasts roughly sixty to ninety seconds. She describes it like a wave rushing though our body. Not just one wave, but many waves. Waves we'd do well to learn to ride. To embrace our feelings we must stay present, experience them, and surf that wave. Unpleasant emotions can be helpful to us if we learn to "move through" them.

Sometimes we can avoid uncomfortable emotions for fear if they start, they will never stop. We can worry they will be too intense and overwhelm us, resulting in us losing control. But if we think of it as a wave rushing through our body that will subside. If we choose to ride the wave and see what it is telling us, if we embrace it and stay fully present, we can move through the emotion and actually gain more control, self-confidence, and strength as a result.

● It's OK to Not Be OK and...

In my opinion, the phrase, "It's OK to not be OK" is both helpful and unhelpful.

I believe it is important to state that emotional pain is valid and not a sign of weakness. It is part of being human. We feel deeply, and the world we are living in is full of sorrow. To experience sadness, fear, confusion, disappointment, anger, and anxiety is inevitable. It is important we don't demand unrealistic optimism from ourselves or others. It can be damaging to overstate positive affirmations. Toxic positivity like that can shut down genuine emotions and lead to secondary ones like shame, embarrassment, and guilt.[28]

It really is OK to not be OK.

In fact, the feelings that are often categorized as "not OK" are necessary to our emotional health, and one could argue they are being misrepresented in the first place. If you are struggling with your mental health, it is OK to not be OK. Surely validating that it's "OK to not be OK" is only part of the process, though?

If someone I love is experiencing uncomfortable emotions, it is good and right to validate those feelings and not allow my personal discomfort to negate their thoughts, expedite their recovery, or imply they are wrong or weak. My part in the relationship is to sit with, to journey with, and comfort. My role is to hold, not drag or push. It would be unkind to dismiss their emotions of anxiety and fear as unfounded. It would also be unkind of me to be content with them feeling that way for a long time.

As previously discussed, emotions pass. Both comfortable ones, like joy and excitement, and uncomfortable ones, like sadness and fear. Emotions are temporary, and there is power in sitting with whatever you are feeling. If you try to suppress your emotions, they may grow and become stronger. Allow them to be and to pass through you. Encourage others' emotions to be and to pass through them, too. It's not that anxiety shouldn't ever be felt. It's that anxiety as a permanent state of being can be unhealthy.

I like to think of it as journeying with my emotions. Passing through a field of sadness, for example, knowing I can walk through it, learn from it, embrace it, and feel it. I don't want to camp there, though. I may even pause and sit for a time, but I don't want to build my house there.

Eventually I need to keep moving, expecting my journey to lead me to a field of "better" on the other side. You may need a professional to walk through your field with you, and that's OK if you do. Reach out to someone who can help you. Let's notice if we've set up camp with our uncomfortable feelings that were only meant as a temporary visit, those feelings that were for our benefit but are now causing us more harm than good because we stayed there longer than we should have.

So, I want to offer:

It's OK to not be OK, and you don't have to stay that way.

When you are ready and know you need to move through your field of "not OK," reach out to people who can help you. Grief, fear, pain, or anxiety may have wrapped themselves around you so tightly you can hardly breathe. Have they become so much a part of your daily life that to remove them feels scary and intimidating? They may take a long time to unwrap, and this will need to be done carefully so as not to cause more damage, but if that comfort blanket stays as it is, it might repel those around you. Harboring heartache and dining out on despair can be a cozy swaddling restricting you from living life to its fullest.

Is your heart is broken? You are not the only one.

Do you have good reason for resentment? You are not the only one.

Are you in physical pain? You are not the only one.

Are you aching in body, mind, or soul?

I am genuinely sorry if you feel that way. You need to know, though, you are not the only one. You are not alone in these feelings. I sometimes feel them, too. Humanity is burdened with pain. It is part of our condition to feel some of these things at some point in our lives.

You are not alone.

The ability to choose our response to those situations is our human superpower. I am humbled by stories of people who have faced utter tragedy and somehow managed to own their emotions and deal with it as best they can.

Resilient Responses

Terry Waite CBE, envoy for the Church of England, was taken hostage from 1987–1991. He had travelled to Lebanon to try to release four other hostages, but he himself was imprisoned. He spent 1,736 days in captivity, blindfolded and alone. He was chained by his hands and feet to a wall for twenty-three hours and fifty minutes of every day. He didn't see sunlight for nearly five years. His story is compelling. I was struck how in one interview he named three things he felt helped him get through his imprisonment:

1. No regrets.
2. No self-pity. "If you're guilty or not, self-pity will kill you. Self-pity is just a killer, you can't afford to go into self-pity. You may not like your circumstances, you may think you've been a damn fool. But self-pity will kill. You've got to throw it out of the door as soon as it comes in."
3. No oversentimentality. "You can't live life again. What has been is with you.... And that was tough."

> "One of the things you've got to realize, regrettably, unfortunately, this is not a fair world. It's not a just world. Everybody does not get the same deal in life."[29]
>
> —Terry Waite CBE

Waite chose what to do with the blanket that was thrown on him. He didn't deny its existence, but he also did not allow it to restrict him any further than was absolutely necessary. One of the ways he retained his dignity while in captivity was by taking his trousers off each night, folding them, and placing them under his pillow so they were pressed for the following day. His captors may have taken away his freedom, but he preserved his self-respect. How utterly admirable.

Amy Morin, author of *13 Things Mentally Strong People Don't Do*, agrees.[30] She believes one of the ways to be strong is to accept that life isn't fair, because it isn't. She points out three unhelpful beliefs, including:

> Unhealthy beliefs about ourselves.
> Unhealthy beliefs about others.
> Unhealthy beliefs about the world.

Morin adds to the weight of wisdom that says the best way to deal with uncomfortable emotions is to feel them and then move on. It is better to have confidence to deal with our discomfort, and self-pity is unhealthy. It takes a lot of work to get rid of unhealthy behavior and focus on the good, but it is worth it.

I'm sorry if I sound less than sympathetic, but honestly, sometimes more sympathy is not what is needed. Sometimes a reality check and a reminder we are in control of ourselves, even if we are not in control of our circumstances, is freeing.

You have the power to control something in your circumstance—you!

It may be that your thinking is your only place of independence left, the final frontier of defense. Be in charge of your thinking. Be in charge of you. Know when you need to sit with your grief, sadness, and anger. It's OK and understandable to feel those things.

When those feelings start to turn on you and do you more harm than good, when self-reflection becomes self-pity to the point that you are sabotaging yourself, notice the blanket. Notice when it has turned from being good for you to being unhealthy. Even the best food may go out of date. When it goes past its best and has gone rotten, it will make you sick if you continue to feast on it.

Choosing to think on what is good and lovely is a little like wrapping a soft, clean, warm blanket around ourselves. We will find peace and calm, even if a storm is raging around us. Sometimes life is simply so grueling it is hard to name things to be grateful for. I have felt devastation to the extent that looking for something to be grateful for was like looking for the sun at midnight. If that resonates with you, may I suggest a starting point?

Notice your breathing right now and express gratitude for it. It is not everyone's privilege to be alive today. You can then, perhaps, go on to make a short list of things to be grateful for.

● Five to Thrive

Check your "five-to-thrive" list, and if you can say yes to one of these things, name it as something to be grateful for:

Are you:

1. Safe?
2. Clean?
3. Warm?
4. Fed?
5. Loved?

You don't have to be liked by everyone—what a relief!

Let's just take a moment to revisit.

"What Does It Matter?" if you expect to be accepted and loved by everyone?

It matters as you may get hurt and disappointed because (and this bears repeating):

People accepting you is as much about them as it is about you.

Even more, it may just be about how they are in the moment of that particular day. Go slowly when responding to people, because you don't know the story behind their story.

If you feel you need to adapt who you are to fit in, go find some other friends. Find people who will call you to greater and better things. A good friend will bring out the best in you, not require you to hide it. A good friend will lovingly point out the rubbish in you and help you clear it up. A good friend will not need to understand you to accept you. A good friend will create an environment for you to be the very best you can be, not a lesser version of yourself to make them feel secure.

Some people don't want to be around me because they say I'm too private. Others think I am too energetic. What have people said about you? I have grown and am learning to deal with it all better. When people say anything like this to me now, I examine my behavior and look to see if I have been overbearing or unkind. I know my "full self" can be a bit full-on and does not need to be present every second of every day! I can see when it is appropriate for people to only see a limited view of me at any one time. It is important, though, that whichever part of myself I am showing be true and authentic.

Therefore, the pursuance of acceptance is exhausting because it is rare for people to both fully know you and fully accept you. It may be a small handful of friends and/or family who accept you. And that's OK. Do be accepted, but be accepted by the few who really matter to you.

If we make acceptance a foundational value in our life, we are putting our foundation in the hands of another human being. Any time we hand over the control of how we see ourselves to someone else, we are on shaky ground. If they adore us, tolerate us, or hate us, it will be as much about them as it is about us.

Stop handing your power over to other people. I believe we should live at peace with everyone as much as we are able to. That doesn't mean losing your own peace in order to chase the affirmation of someone else, though. Being at peace with everyone includes experiencing peace with yourself.

Give yourself a break! Stop expecting 100 percent in your "likability" ratings. In fact, if you are scoring 100 percent, it is possible you are either only spending time with people exactly like you (in which case consider adding some diversity to your companions), or that you just assimilate to whomever is around you, and that's exhausting. Real friends crave authenticity from you.

I believe Jesus is the Son of God. I have close friends who disagree but who believe that Jesus was, at least, a good person. Well, even Jesus wasn't liked by everyone, and he certainly didn't try to please everyone. So, if even Jesus was divisive and hated because he was true to himself, why do you think you would be any different? You don't have to be liked by everyone to be a good person.

Free yourself from the tyranny of wanting to be liked and applauded by everyone. On *Running Wild with Bear Grylls*, season 2, episode 9, President Barack Obama says to Bear:

"I always tell my daughters: 'Don't believe the hype when things are going good, and don't despair when things are going bad.'"

Be yourself and be accepted by a few people who really matter to you. If you are adored or hated by others, "What Does It Matter?" Honestly. Really. "What Does It Matter?"

● The Unexpected

Turner's Oak was created by nurseryman Mr. Turner of Essex, back in the late 18th century. He crossed the English oak with the holm oak and planted it in an arboretum in the Royal Botanic Gardens, Kew, England.

In the early 1980s, some two hundred years after planting, the arboretum team at Kew noticed the tree was not entirely healthy and was contemplating how to sustain it for the next two hundred years.

Then, in the early hours of October 16, 1987, a devastating hurricane hit England. With winds of over 80 mph, it was the worst storm recorded in the last three hundred years. It was unexpected and deadly. The Meteorological Office had said there would be strong winds and showers, but nothing in this realm. The weather forecasters were just as confounded as everyone else. They could see, with hindsight, what had happened, but they were unable to forecast it in advance to give people the warning they needed.

Most of the damage was done during a ferocious four-hour window between 2 a.m. and 6 a.m. The strong winds that had come in from the southwest roared through England, tearing through residential areas and woodlands, leaving a trail of devastation in their wake. Sadly, about fifteen million trees were lost and twenty-two people died. Thousands were left without power for days, and the landscape was changed forever. The southeast was hit the hardest, and people struggled to come to terms with the extensive loss of trees, many of which were historic and had been there for decades, and some for centuries. Trees that had stood proudly among the community acting as landmarks were now strewn like driftwood across the landscape. The familiar horizon had changed shape, and shadows that had travelled through the land like clockwork every twenty-four hours for years would never again take form. The erasing of those recognizable and stunning structures provoked united grief for life and history that could never be recovered.

The Royal Botanic Gardens in Kew was hit hard, and they lost about seven hundred trees within the space of an hour. Those who tended the arboretum were heartbroken as they awoke to the debris and destruction of the aftermath of the assault. Trees that had been lovingly and diligently looked after for years were now felled by the most aggressive hurricane in England in three centuries. Turner's Oak was no different. Along with other trees, it's beautiful canopy had acted like sails in the high winds and it had been lifted, together with its root plate, up and out of the ground before being slammed back in its original position. This magnificent tree was left humbled, slightly tilted, with its roots exposed.

Following the storm, Tony Kirkham, the Head of Arboretum at Kew, carried out a survey of the gardens, assessing the damage of each tree, looking for triggers (such as broken branches, cracks in wood, hanging branches, and complete failure of trees) and working out the plan to either save or clear the trees to make the gardens safe for the public once again. He was devastated by the damage to Turner's Oak and was determined that he and the team would try to save it. They set about propping it up as best they could. Knowing they needed to clear other trees that had fallen, they decided to leave cutting up this historic oak until last.

Over the next three years, Tony and his team cleared the damage left by the storm. Tree after tree was cut and cleared, and gradually the ravaged trees were removed, sadly leaving a dramatically altered vista in their absence.

● Nourished to Flourish

When Tony came back to Turner's Oak three years on, he was amazed to find that it was healthy and thriving. In fact, it was healthier than before the storm. He and his team were both utterly delighted and bemused. How could this tree that had been lifted out of the ground, shaken, and then placed back again survive such trauma? Even its root plate had left the ground and was precariously propped back into position. How was this tree looking better than it did before the storm? Tony and his team set about trying to find out why it had not only survived, but had actually thrived.

Eventually they learned that the root plate coming out of the ground had provided the tree's roots with much needed oxygen and nutrients. Decades of people and animals walking over the ground had led to the soil around the roots being compacted, and this was the cause of the symptoms the team had observed years earlier.

The Arboretum Team had noticed prior to the storm that the oak was looking tired and stressed, they just didn't know how to fix it as they hadn't yet identified the cause of the problem. Many of the trees in Kew were suffering in the same way.

The tree had been stressed and under pressure from the daily activities and rhythm of life. The compacted soil was suffocating Turner's Oak, and it was gasping for oxygen—oxygen that the storm provided.

Now, three years after the storm, Turner's Oak was thriving again. The root plate of the tree had been shaken, uprooted, and had experienced immense trauma caused by an unexpected and uncontrollable force, but the tree was benefitting in the long run. Short-term damage produced long-term health.

The lessons learned from Turner's Oak have been felt all over the world. Those caring for trees now actively ensure that roots are not compacted, and they work hard to aerate the soil. Machinery has even been invented to replicate the effect of the storm, loosening up the soil and reinjecting it with oxygen and nutrients. The storm wreaked havoc, and the loss of millions of trees and wildlife was real and painful. But it was not all bad. The storm was terrible with dreadful consequences, without a doubt. But there was also good that came out of it. Good that couldn't have been predicted and wouldn't have happened otherwise. It brought with it a new way of doing things, a revival of old life, and hope for a better future.

Turner's Oak, a beautiful evergreen, still stands magnificently with its low-lying branches inviting explorers of all ages to have fun and climb through its wise and aging embrace. It has gained more than 30 percent of its growth in the last thirty years and continues to flourish, as do other trees that have benefitted from the knowledge gleaned from Turner's Oak in Kew Gardens.

● Don't ignore the symptoms, even if they are mild.

Where are your roots compacted? Where has the stress and rhythm of life compacted the soil around your roots to the extent that you are suffering a lack of oxygen and vital nutrients? Perhaps you are not quite functioning properly, not totally happy, but it has been hard to pinpoint the exact cause. You can see the symptoms, but not the cause. Perhaps other people can see the symptoms, but you have yet to acknowledge their nagging presence in your day-to-day living. The team at Kew had observed the tree was under stress. They just didn't know how to fix it. The storm provided the solution to a problem they didn't know they had.

Someone recently told me I was infuriating because I always brought every conversation, observation, or comment back to something positive. I am a relentless optimist, and although fun to be around, it does also have its downsides. For example, in business, optimists can too often take risks, overpay people, and not see (or choose to minimize) the threats to the business.

I have realized that I don't tolerate things being bad. I am constantly turning things into something good, constantly seeing the silver lining and always bringing things back to the positive outcome. I don't do this consciously, but I feel the need to see the positive in every situation. Sounds great, right?

But if I never allow something to be bad, I will never try to fix it. I soldier on, tolerating all sorts of things that I have justified as good, or at the very least, found something good in. Soil becomes compacted around my roots as I manage, cope, and tolerate things that are no longer beneficial to me.

Don't get me wrong. We all need to do things that aren't our first choice. I believe those jobs I didn't enjoy were character forming for me. I tell my kids that we all need to do things we don't enjoy when it comes to chores, contributing to the house and our family life. Please don't misunderstand me. I'm not perpetuating a life of hedonism, pursuing only my own joy and filtering my life based solely on what is pleasurable or not. Clearly there is a balance to be had. I'm talking about making the right decisions for the right reasons. You can do something you don't enjoy if the reasons are good.

I need to create opportunities for my root plate to get lifted. To allow oxygen to get to my soil and honestly look at what is good, what is bad, and make some changes before my root plate gets stuffed back into the ground again. Once I have faced the truth, I can muster the courage to do something about it, and muster the courage I must.

Are you doing a job that is suited to who you are now, or who you were? Are you doing a job that is suited to who you are becoming?

Where do you need oxygen?

Are you resting or wrestling? We encounter storms, no doubt. Storms can bring confusion, fear, and agonizingly brutal destruction. We can get lifted from the ground, shaken around, and hurled back to earth again.

Next time you encounter a brutal storm, is there any way you can find something good to glean from it? Some joy, some oxygen, some level of hope? Don't be hard on yourself, though. Remember Turner's

Oak wasn't revived during the moment of the storm. Rather, the storm was the start of its recovery process over several years.

Wake Up

One New Year's Eve we set alarms on our phones and went to sleep. We had diligently packed our suitcases and got everything ready for a very early wake-up call. We needed to be at the Channel Tunnel by 6 a.m., which meant leaving our house at 5 a.m., which in turn meant waking us all up at 4:30 a.m.

Panic jolted us awake just after 5 a.m.

The alarms had failed to sound. We ran around the house, grabbed sandwiches out of the fridge, and threw ourselves into the car. Though grateful we had prepared so well the night before, we were still rattled by what had happened, and we couldn't understand it. For one phone to fail would be peculiar enough, but both? On the way to the port, we heard on the radio that many people across the globe had experienced the same problem. There was a glitch relating to the calendar linked to certain devices, and many had missed their flights and other important events because their phone alarms had let them down.

Humanity likes to feel in control. We set our alarms and choose when to get up. We control the start to our day. That is, unless you are a guardian or parent of small children, in which case they may be your alarm! We feel we are in command of our day, but we can easily forget we are relying on the sun to rise, which is, of course, entirely out of our hands. We may control the small step of our alarm and when we get up out of bed. We may stretch to switch a light on, but there is one significant light well out of reach. We need the sun. When we set our alarms for the morning, we are acting in faith that the sun will rise again. The sun rising is in God's control, and no matter how hard humanity tries, I can't ever see us managing to master that! We are still learning how to look at, study, and perhaps visit different planets and stars. It is unlikely that we will be able to move them any time soon.

How much are we in control, really? The illusion of control is something we mostly find comforting. It is not until we are faced with something beyond our control that we remember we are not in charge of everything, and in fact, there is much in life that we simply cannot steer. If we were to focus on all the areas where we aren't in control, we might freeze in fear. But we can also use this knowledge of being out of control for our good, not harm. There are times when I can relax, knowing that keeping the earth spinning is not in my jurisdiction. There are times I remember to avoid putting energy into something that is out of my control anyway.

Sunrise Series

I regularly post photos of the sunrise on social media in my #sunriseseries. I do this because I recognize that not everyone sees the sunrise. It is easy to get up late and find it is light outside while forgetting the sun rose to make it so. It is a helpful start to my day because the sunrise is consistent. Each day, there it is again. It is at a slightly different time and place as we go through the year, but it is always there.

Consistency is surely lacking in some areas of life as we know it, so to have this constant is helpful and reassuring to me. The sunrise also reminds me to be thankful. Thankful for people, places, things both in and out of my control. It is extremely beautiful, and I often pause in wonder. I just take a few minutes to appreciate the beauty. It is a scene which, on one hand, I have seen many other mornings—the same field, trees, and garden. But, remarkably, it looks different every day. God is never short on creativity; the dawn is painted differently every day, and I appreciate that.

Last, it helps me to put things in perspective. It reminds me I am a tiny human on a spinning planet in an enormous galaxy. I do not know everything, and I can't control everything. It reminds me that the world is much bigger than the square footage of my house, and there are people experiencing all sorts of things I will never see in my lifetime. It sparks gratitude, compassion, and takes the pressure off me needing to be queen and ruler of everything. I don't need to have everything sorted out, and I am OK with being OK.

If you feel the need to control things a little more than is helpful to you and/or others around you, may I suggest you do your own sunrise series? You may not be facing east to see the actual sunrise, but perhaps for a few days you can wake early enough to see the night fade away and make way for the day. You could sit quietly and observe the consequence of moving planets and remember:

1. Consistency

Not everything is chaotic and unpredictable. There are some things that are constant. I find the rhythm of the start and end of each day comforting. The steady dance of the galaxy that has been true since the beginning. Humans watching the sunrise centuries ago were watching the same sun as me. Contemplating the longevity of the sun and planets reminds me of my temporary state. I am here for a breath in the timeline of planet earth. Even the trees in my garden were here before me and are likely to be after. This helps to remove the pressure of needing to know everything and be everything. I am part of the story of humanity, not all of it. I just need to play my part well.

2. Beauty

There is beauty both within and outside of yourself. Pause and wonder. While constant, the sunrise is also a different scene each day. Each day is its own artwork. Each day is unique. Every morning is beautiful and is not the same as the day before. There is no limited amount of beauty available for you to see and reflect upon. Our planet provides the most magnificent art every day.

You live in a gallery. You just need to notice.

3. Gratitude

An attitude of gratitude is good for our well-being. When you greet the dawn, try being grateful for being alive. Your body knew to wake up, and you have breath in your lungs. Take a moment to name and be grateful for the people in your life, the places you have been, and the things you have seen. Choose to recall the good. If you find this hard, perhaps you could write down a few happy memories and have them ready to start each day.

4. Perspective

You are only human. Give yourself a break! You are not in charge of everything. Give yourself permission to relax. Think big, look up. Realize that you are a human being and one of billions on a planet in an enormous universe. You matter and your life matters. Make good decisions that will help you live the day in the best way possible and help others at the same time. Allow a bigger perspective to lift your eyes and the weight off your shoulders. Find motivation and freedom in the amazing potential within you.

Stress Less

"What Does It Matter?" helps us recognize the extent of our own influence. When we accept our limitations, we save energy by not trying to fix something that is not in our hands to fix.

Be released from the burden of thinking the world centers around you and relies on you for its existence. It doesn't.

For example, if your train is running late, it may be infuriating and inconvenient. But, unless you are working for the rail company, it is probably out of your control. So "What Does it Matter?"

Notice what is in your control and act on that. Perhaps you need to make a call to apologize for being late to your destination. Maybe you need to rework your schedule to adapt. These action points help us respond with what is in our power and have a positive impact on the situation. Act on what is in your control.

It is not helpful to get stressed about the train because your stress does nothing to improve the situation. It doesn't matter whether you sit on the train with stress running through your body or not. The train will not go faster for it. Your stress levels will not impact the train schedule. Identify where you can take action and find some rest. Is it possible to sit on the train without a high level of stress? Using the time positively cannot affect the arrival time of the train, but it will directly affect the state in which you arrive.

> What would it feel like for you to surrender control and relax?

When you feel stressed because something out of your control is impacting you (e.g. train is delayed).

● WHAT DOES IT MATTER?

What	What am I feeling? Notice and name your feelings.
Define	What, exactly, is the real issue?
Importance/ Impact	Ask yourself "What Does It Matter?" Be honest about how important the issue is to you. Think about the real impact.
Make a Plan	Choose to act or to let it go.

● Manage Your Stress

What: Feeling frustrated. Feeling stress rising. Feeling regret that I didn't leave more time.

Define: There is an impact on my day, and it is out of my control. I'm feeling embarrassed that I'll be late and annoyed at my lack of control in the situation. I am dependent on others.

Importance/Impact: It really matters to me that I am on time, but that is out of my hands. I cannot change the situation or influence it for the better. The consequence of the delay remains, whether I am stressed or not.

Make a Plan: Take a minute to think about the true consequences (not the overall feeling of "being late" but the specifics). For example, if I am late to that meeting I feel unprofessional, and that I have wasted someone else's time. Then take those specific things and see what you can influence. I will call that person (not text) so there is no miscommunication of the problem and give my sincere apologies. I will give them a new ETA. Or reschedule. I will learn to leave more margin in my schedule between meetings so that I don't feel this level of stress again.

So "What Does It Matter?" What do you expect? Your expectations directly influence how you experience life. Have high expectations of yourself when it comes to the things that matter to you. For me, those are love, patience, kindness, goodness, faithfulness, integrity, hope, and peace. Notice the treasure in your ordinary everyday life. See where you may be able to lower your expectations and take the pressure off. Use "five to thrive" to reassess your priorities and be gentle with yourself. Don't expect to be liked by everyone at all times. You don't need everyone to like you, just a small few who really matter to you. Being liked by everyone is not the sign of a good person. Be true to yourself and expect great things in life, because even the storms can help you thrive over time if you let them.

What Does It Matter?...
...How I See Things?

LET'S GET SOME PERSPECTIVE

....

🔘 In Your Shoes

While songwriting in Sydney, I stayed with a beautiful couple who went above and beyond to host me with grace and generosity. One day I explored the city after a studio session. My host was trying to establish where I had been and she mentioned "the old building" as a landmark. I was genuinely baffled, trying to figure out which building I had seen that was "old." After several moments of confusion, we realized our error. "Old building" to me was very different from "old building" to her.

A few months later I watched my son, dressed in all white, bowl very fast at the opposition and take a wicket. As I absorbed the rare warmth of sunshine in the southeast of England, I observed a plaque that stated the school I was sitting in was founded in 604 AD, and then reconstituted by King Henry VIII in 1542. People have been educated at King's Rochester for over 1,400 years. The school is still very much thriving and served a rather splendid afternoon tea after the cricket! It was awe-inspiring history, thinly veiled by everyday life. When I read the plaque, I recalled the conversation with my host in Sydney who laughed that I didn't know what the old building was. The building she was referring to was less than 150 years old, and there I was, in a school more than 1,400 years old. As a girl growing up in the southeast of

England, my definition of "old" was very different from my host living in Sydney. Same building, different perspective. "Old" is relative.

Have you ever revisited your childhood school to find what you once thought was enormous is, in fact, quite tiny? I have memories of large classrooms and playgrounds and yet, on a visit during adulthood, I realized they weren't large at all. Turns out, I was small. Or perhaps you remember people or places one way, to find that on return, they are quite different than your memory depicted?

We understand ourselves and the world around us based on our experiences, biology, character, and viewpoint. Same world, different take. My dad used to tell me to "put my eternal glasses on." Which basically meant, put it in perspective!

What glasses are you wearing that impact how you see the world? We view the world through a lens that is made up of our experiences, biology, and spirituality. Each human is unique. What is your story, and how does that affect your perspective? What lens are you looking through?

Have you ever found yourself berating a child for being ungrateful for food, pointing out that children in less fortunate circumstances would be thankful? I met children on the streets of Durban in South Africa who would devour food I've seen others push away in disgust. Same food, different appreciation. Food may be less valuable to children who know it is just one of the meals they will be offered that day. To some children sustenance is scarce, to others, it is in abundance. Life-saving treasure to one can be rejected by another. This is not about the monetary value of the food. It is about the value of the food to the recipient, and that changes everything. It differs with each person based on the life they are experiencing and the lens through which they are viewing it.

To try to keep things in a healthy perspective, I regularly ask myself "What Does It matter?" In this instance, I not only ask myself what does it matter to me, but also what does it matter to them? Who is "them"? Well, I think about those children I met on the street who were eating out of trash cans. I think about the young mother I met who, when in labor, had to walk herself to the hospital, gave birth with no one she knew for support, and then walked "home" to the streets once more. Her baby had never known a home other than that of crack houses, alleyways, and curbside cardboard. I think of the family I met who had two adults and thirteen children living together in one very small shack. It consisted of one room that was their bathroom, kitchen, bedroom, and living room. I bring to mind refugee parents so desperate they would choose to risk their family's lives in hope of a safe haven. They set out not knowing how they would survive but convinced the treacherous journey ahead with no shelter, food, safety, or promise was better than staying where they are.

I will never forget a story I heard Preemptive Love founder and CEO Jeremy Courtney tell when he gave an extremely challenging and memorable presentation in London, 2018.[31] He spoke of a mother who needed to escape Syria. She took her child over the mountains, but they didn't have enough water to drink. Every day the child would say: "I'm thirsty," and her heart would break as she would respond with tenderness: "I know, I don't have water yet, but we will." That child's voice got quieter every day until it grew very faint and was eventually a whisper: "Mommy, I'm thirsty." That poor mother had to bury her child on the mountain because she did not have water to quench their thirst. That puts my troubles in perspective.

It is understandable that we find it difficult to relate to the multitude of issues affecting so many different people. But when the issue of a crowd is narrowed down to a single human, a human with a name who has a family, it becomes easier to empathize and harder to ignore.

Compassion Arithmetic

Professor Paul Slovic of the University of Oregon has conducted research around what he calls compassion arithmetic. Sadly, his research findings demonstrate the larger the number of people involved, the less we empathize and activate compassion. To sum up his work, he says the brutal truth is "the more who die, the less we care."[32]

Just take a moment to let that hit. According to latest research, as a general rule:

The more who die, the less we care.

Surely not?! Aren't we caring human beings who believe in the value of life? We see statistics of human tragedy and lose sensitivity as numbers increase. When the numbers are especially large, say in the millions, we lose feeling completely. We don't feel the reality of a million people's situation. We don't care. This is outrageous, and we know it isn't acceptable, so how does it happen?

To empathize is essentially to put ourselves in the shoes of another. To imagine how that person feels. Our brains can instinctively understand what a situation looks like from someone else's standpoint. Granted, there are some who are better at this than others, but humans are usually able to empathize with another to some extent. How, though, can we put ourselves in the shoes of two people at the same time? Our brains find it awkward to grasp the essence of two people at once.

Research shows we lose some degree of empathy trying to understand two people's situations, rather than one. How much more is lost then, when we're asked to put ourselves in the shoes of hundreds of thousands of people? Our brains find it difficult to do. We create what Slovic calls "perverse compassion arithmetic," which makes us think that while one life is extremely valuable and two lives are also valuable, we somehow care a little less if it's two people at risk rather than one. By the time we get to one hundred people, the numbers are so big we find it difficult to put ourselves into their shoes and our compassion decreases. The higher the number of people facing adversity, the less able we are to empathize. We experience what Paul Slovic calls compassion collapse.[33]

Research actually shows that the more who die, the less we care. It's repulsive, but true. So how do we overcome this emotional numbing? How can we combat this non-rational arithmetic? Well, we need to personalize it. We need our rational thinking to help us move away from the numbing information of statistics and back to individual stories. Holocaust survivor Abel Herzberg sums it up like this:

"There were not six million Jews murdered; there was one murder, six million times."[34]

This is important for us when asking ourselves "What Does It Matter?" because we may know we need to put things in perspective, but our brains struggle to look at anything outside our personal world. We live in an age of information about millions of people around the globe. Centuries ago, people's relationship circles were far smaller, and their point of relativity would have been influenced by this relational network. Now, our network is global, and we are connected to people we have never met. We feel the need to respond to people outside our circle of relationship and to circumstances outside our experience. Our global community requires empathy on a global scale, and our brains can't easily handle that. Global statistics can leave us feeling unemotional and disconnected.

We can proactively work against the inability to empathize with many by learning the story of one. If you find it difficult to widen your perspective in a healthy way, can I urge you to do some research and find another individual who is facing hardship that puts yours in perspective? Don't just use them for your purposes, though. Act, donate, communicate, raise awareness, and respond with compassion. Empathy is only one step on the journey. To understand how they might be feeling is important. To act with compassion in response to that understanding is the goal.

ONE

Paul Slovic conducted an experiment where he presented a picture of a seven-year-old child and told people their donations would save her from starvation. Thankfully people donated to feed this poor child. Interestingly, he then asked a second group the same thing, but this time the photo was against a backdrop of statistics showing she was one of thousands of children who were starving. Her story was put in the context of the bigger problem; there were thousands of starving children. Sadly, donations dropped nearly in half when donors knew she was one of many of children.[35]

Knowing about the children they weren't helping diminished the givers' positive feelings of doing good for the one they could feed. The result: They helped less. People were demotivated by the fact that they couldn't help everyone, and donations plummeted. A sense of helplessness doesn't feel good and can often lead to doing nothing rather than doing the small thing that is in our power to do. I wonder if this is an outworking of our global experience (knowing the situation of millions of people in another country) being processed by our "local brains."

Compassion collapse, as Paul Slovic calls it, can be explained by the extent to which our brain finds it awkward to empathize with more than one person. I agree with him that it doesn't make it right, though. It explains, but doesn't excuse.

I believe the majority of people do care. We do want to help. We do love. Yes, it is hard for our brains to compute the circumstances of many, but our hearts want to, and that's what counts. We can use this important research and understanding to drive our brains where we really want them to go. Where our hearts truly are. To help others.

"What Does It Matter?" can act as a gear change, enabling us to experience more empathy and act with more compassion.

● WHAT DOES IT MATTER?

What	What am I feeling? Notice and name your feelings.
Define	What, exactly, is the real issue?
Importance/ Impact	Ask yourself "What Does It Matter?" Be honest about how important the issue is to you. Think about the real impact.
Make a Plan	Choose to act or to let it go.

● Manage your apathy

What: Feeling apathetic about something I know I should care about.

Define: I'm finding it too easy to ignore and feel demotivated to help.

Importance/Impact: This really matters. Millions of individuals need help.

Make a Plan: Make it personal and think of one individual. Help even just one, knowing doing something is better than doing nothing. If many people helped just one person, many people would be helped.

If you feel powerless to help, join forces with charities and NGOs amplifying your efforts by giving your resources—time, money, and strength—to those who have more power. Understanding how we are thinking and behaving helps us to make the world a better place. Ask

"What Does It Matter to them?" next time you are tempted to complain. You may have forgotten to put things in perspective.

Point of relativity matters, and it explains in part why life experience is incredibly helpful to the growth and development of one's character. I remember remarking to my family that since traveling, everything I knew before felt different. My point of relativity had expanded, and my perspective had changed. What I once knew as poverty now didn't look quite so impoverished. What I once knew as generosity still held as that, but I had been exposed to another level of hospitality, of people giving from their lack, as opposed to giving from abundance.

Experiences providing perspective can, of course, work the other way, too. I once had the privileged experience of flying business class. It was brilliant until we flew home economy class on the same trip, and my travel companion spent a good portion of the journey frustrated. They'd tasted luxury, and their frame of reference had changed. What had previously been fun now felt unsatisfactory. They stole a little of the joy by finding the economy return somewhat lacking compared with the luxury outbound journey.

When our experience of life expands, so does our perspective. It takes discipline and insight to develop self-awareness to the extent you can at least recognize the limitations of your viewpoint, even if you cannot fully understand the ramifications of it.

● Comparison Confines

While noticing the lives of others, we may unwittingly stray into comparison. We don't just want to "put on their shoes" and see everything from their point of view. We start asking ourselves how their shoes compare to ours. Feeling we are lacking can lead to upset, hurt, anger, and jealousy. We may get a sense that things aren't how they ought to be. If, on the other hand, we compare shoes and ours look superior—more expensive and better for the road ahead—we could stray into pride and perhaps an unconscious belief that we have more because we deserve more.

Comparison confines, either in self-pity, because we are not as successful as others, or in pride, thinking we are much better than they are. This in turn can unintentionally lead to feelings of superiority and the misconception that there is an unspoken ranking system in humanity where some people are worth more than others.

I believe each human has equal value to another. Regardless of race, gender, sexual orientation, or belief system, humans are valuable. People have different experiences and different opportunities. They have different personalities and respond in different ways. There are currently about 7.8 billion people on the planet, each unique. I agree with some and disagree with others, but we all have the same value and worth as humans. No one person is worth more than another. Some may be better known, but they are not better. Some may be more pleasant to be around, but not more precious. Each human has as much right to be on this spinning ball as any other.

When I am grumbling, I often notice I am striving for something beyond what I already have or have achieved. I am looking for some sense of connection and meaning, perhaps unable to satisfy my desire for significance. I find great peace when I stop, admire, and value what is, rather than what could be. Punctuate your complaining with gratitude and watch it deflate until all there is left is calm.

Complaining holds hands with striving. Gratitude holds hands with peace.

If you start focusing on that for which you are grateful, it is hard to stay miserable for long. I find saying it out loud very helpful. Giving verbal expression to my gratitude is extremely important to me. It influences my thinking, which influences my feelings, which influence my choices for the better.

Thinking – Feeling – Choices

If a hard day for you is one where you feel confused about your future, take a moment to consider a hard day for others is not thinking about the future but their present, how they are going to eat and where they might be able to sleep. One of the best ways I know of putting everything into perspective is asking the question "What Does It Matter?"

Wake Up

In 2020, the world mourned the tragic death of championship basketball player Kobe Bryant. His heartbreaking death, along with his thirteen-year-old daughter punched the world in the face and left it devastated. I didn't know him personally, and I don't know anyone who did, but I felt emotional and extremely sad for his family. I was also conscious of the families of the others in the helicopter crash. Nine people lost their lives. As already discussed, humans have an amazing superpower called empathy that rises to respond with compassion and understanding. I never met Kobe Bryant, but I mourned his loss because I empathized with those who were mourning.

The world was in pain, in part, because it had a brutal reality check that life is temporary. We abhor our own mortality. When we hear of someone who seemed to have it all and who brought so much joy taken too soon, the world suddenly feels less safe, less routine, and more precarious than before. Our perspective has changed. This young, strong, capable, family man lost his life in an instant. It puts every day into perspective because he didn't know that morning was going to be his last. How could he?

Collectively we experienced a heightened awareness of the uncontrollable and awoke once more to the value of those around us. Our perspective changed when we found out the news. But how long did it take to drift steadily back into the sleep of a life more ordinary? How long did it take for us to forget, again, that each day is a gift to be used and celebrated? Kobe Bryant's death was a wake-up call for many. It helped us put life into perspective for a brief time, but in a response similar to the wake-up call from our bedside alarms, how many of us have already drifted back off to sleep again? Are you in "snooze" mode?

The death of someone close to us forces us to view life through a new lens. It acts as a filter, allowing all the worthless drudge to sink to the bottom, leaving the rocks and solid and immovable material at the top. Things that really matter scream for our attention, and a renewed sense of urgency arises, ranging from deep and emotional to seemingly frivolous and adventurous.

Near-Life Experience

Explorer Steve Backshall describes his near-death experience riding rapids in Bhutan as being the best day of his life, even though it was almost his last:

"There is something very liberating about getting a sense of being close to death because it kind of gives you such a greater appreciation of all you have to live for. The sense of gratitude, of friendship, of just how much I owed to these people who are part of my team was massive, was overwhelming and yeah, I will always see that as being one of those big turning points in my life when everything's changed…I had a much greater appreciation of what I had, what I had to lose and what was really important and increasingly that is fatherhood…I think I had always up to that moment been a bit of a searcher…I had thundered around the planet desperately doing all these crazy things in an attempt to find out what I was put here for and I found it in something as simple as becoming a dad. It was such an emotional moment."[36]

I've never personally looked death in the eye and walked away, so I don't have that level of perspective. But how could we all learn from this? Where can we, just with a bit of effort and discipline, choose to extend our boundaries of perspective to do us good and not harm?

What are you waiting for?

It was a cold autumn day when, once again, I stood by my mom's grave with my husband, talking about how life on earth was so short. We recalled that we had always wanted to go to New York but hadn't yet been. I think we'd talked about it for ten years at that point. So right there and then, we committed to go before the next time we were at her graveside. And we did. Every time I am at her tombstone, I am reminded of how brief life is, and I leave with a revived sense of urgency to do what is important to me: to love better, live better, invest in relationships, and leave the world a better place for me having been here.

What are you looking at?

My eyeline changes depending on the terrain on which I am running. I recently started a very familiar route but, in true Emma fashion, decided to let my curiosity lead the way, and I found myself running a path I had never run before. It was thrilling for me to explore woodlands I didn't even know were there. One section of the route was extremely narrow. I'm not sure the rugby-playing, broad-shouldered husband of mine would have been able to walk forward. He'd have probably had to slide along sideways like a crab! The ground was particularly gnarly, with tree roots weaving along the way, mostly embedded for decades. Some poked through the topsoil just enough to create an obstacle course that had me running with "knee highs" like those I've seen at boot camp in army movies! A babbling stream ran alongside, and the path became even narrower when a branch at chin height reached to block my way. It was utterly delightful. It took focus to maintain my speed while not hurting myself. I looked directly down at the ground and glanced occasionally ahead to see the trees I needed to navigate. I was only able to look a few feet in front of me and remained totally focused in the moment to keep my pace up. I concentrated entirely on the placing of my feet. I was ducking and diving between the branches, not unlike a boxer avoiding the right hook of oncoming trees.

It occurred to me that if I looked far in the distance, it would not have been helpful. Neither was looking at the sky, looking behind to see where I'd been, or even worse, having my eyes shut to accentuate the rhythm of my run. It was crucial I looked in the right place at the right time to maintain my pace and stay safe.

I leapt over a stile, and the pathway widened into a field. Suddenly, I lifted my gaze, looked forward, took in the blue sky and became distracted by sheep. Losing myself in wonder in that moment was compelling. My sight line was wider and higher as my next steps were less vulnerable than before. I was able to lift my chin from my chest, look ahead, and take in the landscape when only minutes before, my concentration had solely been on my next few steps. As the terrain changed, so also could my line of vision.

In life, it is imperative to look at the right thing at the right time. Sometimes being absorbed in what you are doing, not just day by day but hour by hour or minute by minute is vital. Just keeping going takes full attention, focus, and detailed analysis. Sometimes it is simply about making the next big or small decision. It may be a focused few hours without phone distraction for dinner, bath, and bedtime with the kids, or a morning that requires your full attention to pass the interview and get your dream job. Spotlighting intense tasks for intense times is helpful. To "just do" what's in front of you in the present and to the best of your ability is both effective and releasing. Other times, though, we can take a breath and pause in wonder. We can look ahead, dream, and see the bigger picture.

Ask yourself "What Does It Matter?" Where does my focus need to be today? When feeling overwhelmed I find that focusing on just that particular day is extremely helpful. To hone my vision down to the next minute, the next hour, and the present helps me manage my to-do list and emotions. Less pressurized times can feel a little more like open space. I am able to lift my eyes, look up and out, see the bigger picture, and focus on the way ahead. For those of us fortunate enough to experience vacations, I think this is what happens when we are away from our rhythm and routine. We step away from the commute or the school run and have a chance to look at the wider things, the bigger things. By stepping further away from our everyday life for a few days, we see it in the distance, and in so doing, we gain a new perspective. It is important to be aware of your viewpoint and how it influences everything else.

● Victory Over Victim

I am not an expert at this, but here are a few examples where I have been helped by putting things in perspective. Perhaps you can use these, too, or at least they may suggest similar scenarios for you. Expressing sadness, anger, frustration, or other uncomfortable feelings can be a signal to me that either my attitude or circumstances need to change. I actively address the unnecessary complaining in myself that is making me feel worse and not better, the type of complaining that overshadows the good and highlights the challenging.

Here are some examples:

1. When relentless demands from my children leave me feeling tired, I might think what it would be like to lose them. It only takes a teeny tiny moment to imagine life without them, and I feel desperately grateful for them again! The turnaround on this one is both dramatic and instant. Tiredness is temporary. My deep love for them is forever.

2. We moved from our home with a large fridge to one that had very limited capacity. This sounds like a minor thing, and it is. The reason I had to discipline my perspective was because it affected every single day. I spent time needing to shop more often than I wanted. The fridge was too small and didn't work properly. It really wasn't sufficient for the job. We didn't own the house and kitchen appliances, so our options were few.

Noticing a pattern of complaining developing, I planned to counteract it. I decided that when I whined about my fridge being too little (grumbling in my head or out loud), I would instead turn my focus to the food being too plentiful. I did this often and exchanged frustration for humility. Squeezing the next meal into our fridge transformed from being a problem to an opportunity to be thankful. One perspective leads to self-pity, the other to gratitude.

3. When I complain, often mumbling under my breath, I purposely look at my language and scan how many times I used the word I. It helps me realize much of my bewailing comes from a self-centered viewpoint, and if I stop centering everything around me, I'd feel better.

4. If I'm tired on the way back from work, I may express exhaustion but will always quickly follow with "at least I've got work." This doesn't negate my valid feeling of tiredness. It simply places it in a context where I can be grateful for the cause of that fatigue.

5. When cleaning our toilets, I resist the urge to mutter a complaint by thinking of the many people across the globe who do not have sanitary provision.

You get the idea. I know this may sound pompous, but I honestly use this system to try to fight against the temptation to behave like a selfish, spoiled brat. When I flip a viewpoint on something like this it can often feel manufactured, but that doesn't seem to matter. It still works! Even if I am forcing myself to say something I don't truly feel, the very act of saying it means I start to feel it. I fool myself out of discontent.

If one pain point regularly rears its head, I assess if it needs to stay that way or whether it is in my control to change or influence it for the better. Noticing low-level grumbles about small things can lead to a big pressure release if I act to change them. Perhaps there are a few very simple changes you can make that will leave life working a little easier for you, helping you to minimize your moaning?

You don't have to put up with something by finding the good in it all the time. You could just change it and reduce your angst that way. I realize this seems obvious, but for me there are times I have tolerated something that needn't be tolerated, simply because I forgot it was in my power to change it. I remember complaining about a frying pan that was difficult to use because it had lost its nonstick surface and was so beaten up it wasn't flat anymore. One day I saw pans on sale and bought myself a new one. I remember laughing and thinking: "Why on earth didn't I do that earlier?" Many people I know have told me of similar examples. We tolerate so many tiny but irritating things that could simply be addressed by making a small change.

If you see a pattern to your complaining, either change the thing you are complaining about or your attitude. But do change something, for everyone's sake!

Perhaps take a moment to see where a change of perspective would be helpful and make a note of it so when you next find yourself feeling a certain way, you are ready with a healthy response—a response that doesn't deny your feelings, but that helps you to carry them better. Don't rely on your spontaneous response, as you may be tempted to be led by your feelings, and your feelings aren't facts. I find planning for emotional responses and feelings is widely underused. We are often encouraged to plan for events, opportunities, achievements, and purchases.

> But when was the last time you planned for your feelings?

When did you plan a response that sets you up for the life you really want? Do you plan for a response that shapes you to be the person you really want to be? To be the person you are becoming?

I love the story of Winston Churchill, sitting in the back of a taxi at 10 Downing Street, writing on some note cards before entering an event. When asked by the driver what he was doing he simply said: "I'm just preparing my impromptu remarks."[37]

Prepare your anti-complaining remarks. Spot your complaining triggers and think of another angle that counteracts that stinking thinking. Know where your weak points are and make a plan for them. I feel better when I do. There are a surprising number of patterns in our behavior, and if you notice them, you can set yourself up to win. Know yourself, and in doing so, help yourself.

Confidently Wrong

Our experience affects our mindset, often without us even being aware. A classic example of this was on that same writing trip to Sydney. I was overjoyed to explore the city and find my way around on my own. I love this kind of scenario. Figuring out public transport, maps, and landmarks. I diligently researched a route that morning and confidently set off on my adventure. I was heading to dinner with friends but was making my own way there and relished the solitary time in a new place.

I headed through the city with plenty of time to spare. I decided to go to the harbor sooner rather than later, always preferring to be early. I successfully found the dock and schedule for the ferry and, according to my map, I could take this ferry and then a leisurely coastline walk to the restaurant. Great! I chatted with a chap who said the next ferry was leaving for my destination in thirty minutes. Perfect. An unexpected downpour of rain ushered me under a canopy to drink my coffee and savor this moment of the unknown. I thought about my daily rhythm and routine in familiar places, and how I love the new and unexplored. I committed to continue to purposely look for the unknown in everyday life. It wasn't cold, and the rain soon stopped, with beautiful blue skies returning by the time I got on the boat. I took a seat among businesspeople and tourists. The ferry was full, and the atmosphere was buzzing. The weather was glorious, and the skyline of the harbor was breathtaking. I enjoyed the ride with wind sweeping through my hair and warm sunshine on my face.

I arrived at my destination and confidently disembarked. It was only as the ferry pulled away I realized I was the only person who had alighted at this stop. This surprised me, but a check of the map on my phone was reassuring. I couldn't find my way to the path, so I stopped at the tourist office. As I approached they looked bewildered to see me. I explained where I wanted to go and asked for help.

"Well, you can't get there from here. This is Cockatoo Island. The only way off Cockatoo Island is by ferry. Fortunately, the next one is in twenty minutes, and that's the last one of the day, so you are lucky!"

What? Cockatoo Island is...an island?

Some of you are now thinking I'm bonkers for not realizing that Cockatoo Island is, in fact, an island! But please take into account my experience. I travel in London all the time. I had recently completed a train journey from Bat and Ball to Elephant and Castle and there were no bats, elephants, castles, or balls involved! There are some very peculiar names in public transport in the UK: Oxford Circus is not a circus, neither is Piccadilly. Shepherd's Bush is not a bush, Chalk Farm is not a farm, and if you go to East India, you are probably talking about the dock rather than the country. My experience clouded my judgement, and I mistakenly assumed Cockatoo Island was simply a name of a port, not an actual island. Hilarious!

Turns out, my map app was incorrect at the time, and my mistake is a common one. Apparently the previous time it happened, a group that was trying to get to a wedding arrived on the last ferry and had no hope of a quick escape. Sadly, they all missed the wedding. Travelers regularly get stranded on Cockatoo Island. I laughed hard at myself as I got on the next ferry and off the island. It was fun to have gotten it so tremendously wrong. How did I overlook it was an island? I missed this important information because I was influenced by my experience of random names in London. Never underestimate how your experience affects your everyday choices and way of seeing things.

Of course, our question of "What Does It Matter?" is a trusted framework to put things in perspective. It creates time to engage your rational thinking. It asks a question we all need to ask to find our own, unique answer—an answer that is bespoke to us because what matters to you may be different than what matters to me. Our life experiences create different lenses through which we see life. We do, though, need to know what matters to us and how to respond to it for ourselves.

What Does It Matter?...
...How I Spend My Life?

IT'S YOURS TO SPEND

....

🔘 Memory Lane

I wandered through my old university town with a mix of emotions. Memories came flooding back, nearly all of them good. I remembered feeling extremely emotional saying goodbye to my dad on my first night there. We both had tears in our eyes, and I remember roller-coaster anticipation as I closed the extremely heavy wooden door and walked up three flights of stairs to my little room. I sat on the bed and thought: "Right. What next?" I contacted a friend in the city and arranged to go out that night. It was dark, my first time riding a bike in a city, and I didn't have a clue where I was going. I panicked. Really panicked. Breathless, I turned my bike around and retreated to my room, deciding that my first venture into the city was probably best done in the daylight anyhow. I remember the fear of being utterly lost and feeling quite alone. I got a good night's sleep, woke up, and tried again the next day.

Memories continued to flood in as I saw the shop where I bought my first posh dress for a ball. We had been excited because it was on sale, and we thought it looked great. Looking back on the photos, I believe we were mistaken, but nevertheless, as my first grown-up dress it has a special, if somewhat misjudged place in the wardrobe of my heart. I punted down the river many times while a student. One special time was at dawn, eating a champagne breakfast with strawberries. If you make it to 6 a.m. at a ball, you are named a "survivor," and we were proud survivors of St. John's College Ball. It was all a fairy tale as Nik gave me his tuxedo jacket to drape over my cold shoulders and we ate breakfast gliding down the river, dreaming of our future together.

My old punting company still had crew taking people up and down the river. I was terrible at this job. I mean, terrible! For starters, you had to win the customers yourself by touting on the bridge, and quite frankly, that's a disaster for me as I find it hard to ask for even a cup of tea. Once I finally had customers, we would then head down to the punts and off we'd go. To weave an interesting and exhilarating narrative through the history of such a remarkable institution was easy. Highlighting the study places of poets such as Lord Byron, copious prime ministers, multiple monarchs, the writer of Winnie the Pooh, and the guy who invented the sandwich, what could go wrong? Royalty, scientists, novelists, politicians, philosophers, artists, actors, and architecture. Love, intrigue, historic world-changing movements, and people. Yes, the chat was easy. The punting, though, was a different story.

Two particular occasions stand out for me. One was heaving a boat full of large American tourists. Each of the five people in the boat were at least double my weight and a rather unhelpful current was whirring its way past King's College. Another crew member warned me of the current, but I wasn't strong enough to handle it, so they came alongside me (with their boat of customers also), and we had to ask everyone to hold on tight to each other's boats to tether us together. My crewmate effectively towed us back. I made grand gestures of us working together, mentioning teamwork more than once, but he and I both knew my contribution was minimal, and I was extremely grateful for his rescue! Our customers were gracious, and I remember being humbled by the tip they gave me. It meant a lot to me that they were so generous and understanding.

Another time I tried to untangle the rope that was mooring punts together. Watched closely by my customers, I stood on my punt and stretched out to the adjacent empty one to untie us. I was flabbergasted as the punts serenely parted ways, and I was left stretched belly to water!

I couldn't possibly let go, as I would certainly have ended up in the river. Neither was I strong enough to pull them back together again. In that moment, right next to world-renowned Mathematical Bridge (a feat of meticulous engineering in 1748), I unintentionally created the lesser known Belly Bridge (a result of a spectacular mishap). Time seemed to stand still as I tried to wiggle my way out of my predicament. Eventually someone came to my rescue and pulled the boats together for me. I was very sore and a bit embarrassed, so I tried to style it out. Hilarious! Thinking about it, I hadn't yet learned to laugh at myself in the same way I can now. The punting company swiftly moved me away from the river and into office work.

The fruit and vegetable market where I used to buy my fresh produce had been knocked down and replaced by a very swanky shopping center. In fact, there is an entirely new mall where there used to be some questionable efforts of shop fronts and dodgy alleys. The market square is still there, as are the railings on which I used to lock my bike. The memory of my first argument with my husband flooded back. It was in this moment we learned he was a verbal processor and I was definitely a "walk away-er." I wanted to go and sulk, think it through, and then come back with everything fine and dandy. He made it quite clear that he was not going to stand for that, and it was not over until we had fully processed the disagreement and agreed to disagree at the very least. We have been extremely happily married for a long time, and I have to say that most of the time we resolve issues in his way more than mine, and I am grateful he taught me to express myself more freely. Storming off was dramatic and felt good at the time, but rarely actually resolved anything. I think we now have "our" way of resolving arguments as opposed to that first instance, where we definitely had differing approaches!

As I walked past Senate House, I remembered my graduation ceremony and a sense of pride washed over me. I had achieved something important to me that could not be revoked. Historic buildings still stand magnificently, owning their place in the landscape, confident they deserve to be there and always will. They were there for centuries before me and will likely be for centuries after. Some shops are the same, some altered. The old cobbled streets are unchanged and so is the bike shop where I went for the repairs those old cobbled streets demanded. I loved a certain bench on the lawn of Trinity College along "The Backs." I would retreat there whenever I needed to ponder. The bench was still there, but has been moved ever so slightly down the pathway. A little like me.

The University of Cambridge is made up of thirty-one colleges. Your college is where you live, eat, and build community with people studying different disciplines across the university. Your learning, however, takes place in your faculty, which is a subject-specific community that often has its own location and is made up of people from across all colleges studying in a similar field. Intercollege competition is real and highly competitive.

I am a member of Clare Hall, and as a student I wanted to represent my college in rowing. Now, I am fit and sporty, but I am not designed for rowing. At all. I am way too short, and my legs really don't have the length needed to produce the power required. I was the women's captain purely because I was enthusiastic, but it was evident enthusiasm and ability do not always align. I tried to cox because I was the perfect size for that, but one unforgettable morning, I ended up with our novice boat wedged widthways across the river. We became an irritating dam on an exceptionally busy morning, with boat traffic piling up on either side of us. I desperately tried to figure out how you do what felt like a ten-point turn, calling at eight rowers on a narrow part of the river. On our arrival back to Clare Boat House, we all agreed I was better in a rowing seat than the driving one. I put myself in a position in the boat where I could do as little damage as possible, but where my sheer excitement and drive to be there added a little something to the energy of the boat.

I loved waking up on training mornings, which were often very dark and cold, getting down to my bike and heading off to the river. We needed to be at the boathouse by 7 a.m., and the city was mostly silent.

The draw of fresh air and exercise got me up, but the magnetic pull of team was my main motivator. If even one of the eight people booked in to be at training was a no-show, the boat couldn't go out. We were all compelled to get up because we didn't want to let anyone else down. As captain, it was my job to organize the training roster, and I remember once or twice realizing I was low on numbers and calling friends from other colleges to step in and help us. Where to put the enormous male rugby player I had convinced to come into our all-female boat was a challenge as the stroke of the person in front of you has a massive impact on your own, so I needed to be both persuasive and creative!

One university memory for me was when together with some friends, I climbed over an enormously tall, spiked gate to go and lie in the middle of a field during an electric storm. It was exhilarating and a stupid thing to do, but we were young, naive, and believed ourselves invincible. On the way back, we had to launch ourselves over the gate again, but this time I got myself impaled. My short skirt was caught on the spike, and it took several seconds of swinging rather inelegantly to figure out why I hadn't hit the ground and was still floundering midair. Fortunately, the hem of my skirt was strong enough to hold my weight so I hadn't fallen, but neither could I get myself up and off the spike. I was there for some time, dangling like a puppet and laughing hysterically while my friends decided if they were going to step in and help. I couldn't lift myself off the spike, because there was no leverage for me to push on, so I simply swayed back and forth. Eventually one of my friends lifted me off the gate, but honestly, if they'd run off, I absolutely would have been stuck. There was no way that I could have rescued myself. We ran from there to the tower of my college and finished watching the thunderstorm.

Cambridge is a breathtaking city, and I rarely grew complacent living there. I would routinely look up, breathe it in, and whisper a prayer of thanks for living and studying in such a beautiful and inspiring place.

Same but Different

During the visit I was struck how much had stayed the same and yet how much had changed. Life had moved on at a tremendous pace while at the same time standing still. The paradox of a transient life, changing environment and culture, in among the steadfast and unchanging landmarks and traditions really struck me: Undergrads are not allowed cars in the city, and everyone is still on bikes, except this time I heard someone shout, "Hey Siri…" as they cycled past me. Same scene with significant change.

I reflected on how that was also true in my life. In some ways I have grown and moved on. I have experiences now I didn't have then. I have two children, a husband, and a hamster. I have eaten countless meals and travelled to many different countries. I have met literally tens of thousands of people. I have lost loved ones and gained others to love. Things have changed. I've changed. The passing of time is evident both in everything around me and even on my skin.

And yet, there is also much that seems unaffected by time. I still have a giddy expectation of the world as I walk the cobbled streets with a knapsack on my back. I still have high hopes for my future and optimism for what lies ahead. I still adore my husband and would choose him all over again. I still love being with people, and I love exploring and value my independence. I am still sporty and prioritize exercise. I thrive on learning and blossom when faced with a challenge. I am happy to be confused and happy to work things out. I am, mostly, content.

Walking through Cambridge that day left me with a new sense of forward momentum and at the same time a sense of staying still. Life is a mystery of consistency and change.

Growth and Change

I believe there is a difference between growth and change, and sometimes it is too easy to unwittingly box them as the same. Change can be complete and finite, making things new and even making things entirely different. We can achieve this with our circumstances. We can move house and our home is new. We can change job, location, or car, and what once was, no longer is.

But growth somehow is different. What once was, still is. It may have adapted and evolved. It may have morphed so much it could never truly revert to its original state, but it is still that original material. The beginnings of it are part of its story; they are part of the new.

I think this is like our human experience. We evolve. We grow, and our past is certainly part of who we are, but it does not necessarily have to dictate our future. People try all sorts of different environmental changes in an effort to improve their happiness. Sometimes that is helpful. I remember doing a job where I cried all the way there and all the way home because I hated doing it so much. It took an enormous amount of energy, grit, and determination to get myself into work each day. When I made the decision to do something else, I felt utter joy and relief. I walked differently, felt differently, thought differently, and ultimately, lived differently. There are times when a change is called for, and change at these times can have an enormously positive impact on our well-being. Sometimes, though, what is called for is less of a new start and more growth from where we are.

New Year, New You

"New Year, New You" is clearly a catchy marketing slogan that is easy to remember and has probably generated a lot of revenue. It isn't true, though. I think this phrase can sometimes be unhelpful in setting unrealistic expectations for people. However we change, whether that be in weight, education, hair color, fitness, lifestyle, and so on, we are still the same person, but that person has evolved. I think this is so much more powerful and demanding of respect than the idea that we simply ditch the old person we once were and step into a new version of us. You may have grown so much that you are unrecognizable from the person you were. But you carry all those previous experiences with you. They help to make you who you are.

The other reason this phrase jars against my respect for humanity in all our weirdness, unpredictability, fallibility, and love is that it suggests change can happen almost overnight. There is often an immediacy inferred to promised results, and yet our wonderful and amazing growth is often step by step. We evolve day by day.

Be the Best You

"Be the best you." I mean, come on. The idea of there being a "best" me is ridiculous because it suggests it is finite and attainable. That there is somehow a "best" version of me, just waiting to be found. That if I only managed to live better, do better, work harder, rest more, find peace, eat healthily, and spend a fortune on my appearance, I could manufacture the best version of myself.

I do want to fulfil my potential, for sure. But what happens when that dream you identified as fulfilling your potential is complete? Then what? You dream another dream, you expand, you grow. And suddenly the "best you" you envisaged is only part of the story. It is in your rearview mirror, a punctuation mark in your life's paragraph. There is so much more. You may find "Be the best you" motivating. I, though, find it puts me on a treadmill of pursuit because it is, essentially, unreachable. It is never-ending, and the minute we think we've arrived, we can lose purpose and fall into the "not best" version of ourselves again!

Now, I agree there are days when I am good fun (a better version of me) and days when I am unpleasant (the not-so-good version of me). Of course, I want to aim for more of the fun days than the bad. But please don't harness me with the idea there is somehow this wonderful, best version of myself I could be proud of, if only I improved. I am human, and I mess up. I am human, and my house is sometimes untidy. I am human, and I am older today than yesterday. I am human, and I need to adapt to circumstances and people around me. I am human, and I need community. I am human, and I feel shame and guilt. I am human, and I feel passion. I am human, and I grieve. I am human, and I celebrate. I am human, and am capable of belly laughing one moment and being brought to tears the next. I am a human, full of joy and wisdom, full of hope and love. I am human.

I don't need a marketing slogan to sell an ideal version of myself to myself. Humans grow and evolve, and yes, we

> I am human; stop trying to make a product out of me.

want to improve, but let's be kind to ourselves. There is no "best" you. Aiming for it will be like trying to aim for a moving target. There are situations both in and out of our control. Do try to do your best, for sure. But don't be too hard on yourself if you haven't reached perfection just yet.

Personification

It amazes me that in current marketing trends we tend to personify objects. Whether that be drink packaging printed with "Shake Me" written on the side or a house that has recently been sold having an "I'm Taken" board outside. I've got to be honest, it drives me nuts. And the reason it drives me nuts is that while we are giving inanimate objects personalities and listening to what they "say" to us, we are often dehumanizing humans. Surely we have this entirely the wrong way round?

We personify merchandise and make real people into products. A friend of mine was shocked when I said this at dinner recently. She likes the cheeky conversation she has with her carton of orange juice in the morning, so I realize I may be alone in this. Or perhaps you haven't ever noticed it? I stand firm, though, that in my opinion, it is madness to be personifying stuff. And it is far, far worse to use people as if they were a product.

● Revolving Evolving

I can see where I have changed since I was at university. I have aged, but I'm still fit and healthy. I know more of what I don't want to do but sometimes fumble in the dark about what I do want. I value my time more, and gratitude is part of my everyday life. I can certainly laugh at myself more than I did then, and I don't worry what people think of me to the same extent. Or rather, I do worry what people think, but am choosy about who has a voice in my life and who doesn't.

This sense of staying the same and yet moving on haunts me. Some moving on I am grateful for. I now have a car that will start in the morning regardless of the weather through the night. I can even drive around corners without water pouring in from the ceiling and soaking my right or left leg, depending on my direction. Some changes are good.

Others changes make me wince a little. Not because I massively regret how I have used my time, but because I know I cannot use the time again. Some moments of my life have been written in water and some in stone.[38]

Things have changed, and things have stayed the same. We are like a vapor. Here one day and gone the next. When I was a student, it felt like everything was possible, everything was open to me. It felt like I had all the time in the world. Now I have less time ahead of me than I did then. If I were to leave the earth today, what would be my impact? What would be my legacy? How would anyone know I had been here? Would I have left the world a better place than I entered it?

Our mandate in my business is that everyone should leave the room feeling better than when they entered. Whatever the context. Whatever the cause. My challenge to myself is: Will I leave the world better than it was when I arrived?

Your Life is a Work of Art

We paint the colors, shades, definition, and nuances of our lives. We decide what goes in the foreground or the background. We decide how much attention to give one thing and not another. Drawing in pencil keeps our options open, to allow for changes, backtracking, and erasing what we said or did. When we draw in pen, it is far harder to reverse. There is more commitment to the outcome, and it is almost impossible to hide the mistakes. Pen is braver than pencil. Pencil can be more exciting than pen.

I have, on numerous occasions, been handed opportunities that have disappeared without being fully realized. In hindsight I can see it was my lack of willingness to commit. I didn't choose a direction and put my full force behind it. I tried to continue in pencil when writing in pen would have been more beneficial.

Do you ever find yourself in that situation? Keeping your options open to the point where all options eventually close on you? Or is that just me? If we write in pencil too often, we can end up with a blurry mess on tear-soaked paper, unable to remember what the picture was meant to look like in the first place. Are you writing in pencil, pen, paint, water, or concrete? How we live and the decisions we make will determine the artwork of our life after we've gone.

I wonder if we often put too much energy and time into decisions that are written in pencil as if they were written in concrete. We work ourselves up and expend a huge amount of emotional energy over things that will be a distant memory in a few weeks. This is exactly where we need to be asking "What Does It Matter?"

There is freedom when we realize the temporary nature of our decisions or actions. A weight can be lifted when we realize the thing we are wrestling with really doesn't matter that much.

> To figure out whether your situation is a "writing in water or stone" moment, pause to ask "What Does It Matter?"

Manage your level of commitment by using the WDIM framework to help guide your actions.

WHAT DOES IT MATTER?

What	What am I feeling? Notice and name your feelings.
Define	What, exactly, is the real issue?
Importance/ Impact	Ask yourself "What Does It Matter?" Be honest about how important the issue is to you. Think about the real impact.
Make a Plan	Choose to act or to let it go.

Manage Your Commitment

What: Feeling indecisive.

Define: Could be anything—a decision with long-lasting consequences or a decision that will be unimportant tomorrow.

Importance: It is important to work out the significance and permanence of the consequence of the decision to invest the proportionate amount of energy into it.

Make a plan: Decide if it is a water or concrete moment. If it is water, just act quickly; it probably doesn't matter too much. If it is concrete, act wisely, knowing the implications of your decision will last.

We can become more focused when we realize the action we are taking is significant. Those things written more in concrete than water have significant ramifications that last for a long time. These are the moments worth our full contemplation and attention. They are worth erasing the unimportant pencil moments in order to give our full self to the situation.

Proud of Your Artwork?

When you reflect on your life, will you be pleased with your painting? It's no one else's to paint. There are things that happen that you can't control. Coffee spilled over it, mistakes and tragedy that leave tears and indentations you would rather have avoided, but it is your choice how you respond. You can either weave accidents and mistakes in, making something beautiful, or you can choose to never paint near those damaged areas and leave them alone. Do you avoid pain, leaving a blank canvas surrounding that one moment that forever changed your picture and, sometimes, unwittingly, redefined the boundaries of your life?

We need to regain the revelation that our lives, for the most part, are our choice. You can feel hemmed in by your job, your family responsibilities, and restrictions, but in fact, some of that is down to unspoken cultural expectations.

The unsaid notion of western education is to get educated for "the workplace." Some schools may be bold enough to state they educate "for life." But the system of learning and regurgitating knowledge sets us up to pass exams and does not necessarily set us up for life. I read a list of visiting speakers to talk about career pathways in a school, and there wasn't an "out of the box" job title among them. No entrepreneur or artist. No ethical revolutionary or philosopher. Just doctor, banker, lawyer, and the like. There is nothing wrong with these professions, and I for one am very grateful for the people who do them. I am, though, challenging the assumption that the ideal life, the one well-lived, is one that follows the unspoken rules of a western society. One that studies hard at school, gets great exam results, goes on to university, gets a traditional job, works their way through life, and retires to find they are closer to death than they'd like to admit. Is there more?

It takes courage to dream about what our ideal lifestyle would be. You need to be brave to ask yourself if the life you are living is really the life you want. If we honestly assess our situation, we may realize we have been investing in things that don't matter to us that much. This is difficult to admit but really important to acknowledge and change, if need be.

Our human drive is to be significant. To be noticed, to matter, to be seen, understood, and remembered. If you knew there was no tomorrow, how would feel about yesterday?

Bank of Breathing

Life on earth is like a pot of money. It is finite. It has limitations. What you spend it on matters. You cannot get it back, and you cannot spend someone else's. The kicker of it all is that you don't know how much there is to spend, so you can't save up, plan, and invest. There could be twenty years, forty years, ninety years or more. We don't know. It would be sad to live at a pace that assumed you had more to spend than you actually do. I want to be all used up, and so I embrace each day, week, and month as it is given to me.

Rather than seeing this finite, unknown quantity of time as a bad thing, how about you see it as exciting? You have time, you have days to spend. How brilliant.

Not everyone has the privilege of being alive today, so what will you spend your day on? What do you want to purchase with your time? Your time is more valuable than all your possessions put together. It doesn't matter how much money you have, you cannot increase your number of hours in a day. You can apportion your time differently. You can use it in a new way to free up otherwise allocated time for something else, but you cannot gain time. A lot of other things can be expanded. I remember a particularly wealthy gentlemen once said to me: "The unfair thing is that money makes money. The more money you have, the more money you can make." That is not so with time. You cannot "make time." The size of your car or house, your possessions, your salary. These things can, with intentional effort, change. But not time. You are unable to increase it, stretch it, or buy more of it. You have what you have. Something that not everyone has, you cannot buy, and you cannot increase feels pretty special doesn't it? We should value it. Treasure it. Protect it and spend it wisely.

Too often, I rush through my hour, my day, my week, and my month without appreciating every precious moment of this dear life. The seconds turn to minutes and the minutes to days. We influence our overall experience of life in the hour-by-hour choices we are making.

Of course, big changes and transitions are adventurous and exhilarating. They can make a big impact. And they do. Our location, our house, and our jobs all affect our life. But those spaces we inhabit will continue to feel the same if we live our minutes in the same way. "What Does It Matter?" if you change location, but you yourself remain unchanged? "What Does It Matter?" if you swap your job, but you still feel enslaved to the rhythm of someone else's expectations? How can you carve out a rhythm of daily life aligned to your own values?

Minute by Minute Matters

How we treat each other and ourselves in the minute by minute matters. It's these small specks that make up the painting of our life. If we take the time to look at what truly matters, we must look at the choices we make in our minutes, hours, and days, or else, when we step back and look at the entire picture of our lives, we can feel disappointed by the painting and not understand why. When we look at the strokes of paint, the content and the attitude in which we painted it suddenly becomes clear. We paint our life minute by minute. Not year by year. A lot can change in a year. A lot can change in one moment, actually.

The time we spend is minute by minute. Do you ever think how you may be able to make the next five minutes more enjoyable? Try reducing your time into smaller amounts. To make "life" more enjoyable can feel an impossible task. But if you make your minutes more enjoyable, they will lead to a better life. If you want to change your destination, change your journey. If you want to influence the outcome, influence the process.

> If you want to spend your life well, spend your individual days well.

Our life is the most precious nonrenewable resource. It is up to us to choose what we do with it. We own our bodies, our minds, and our souls. Most of us get to choose what we think about, who and what we celebrate, what we reject, who we spend time with and, to some extent, what we do for a living.

Variability of Environment

We are all walking the same journey on earth, but we all start in different positions on the road. There are variables of opportunity, wealth, and education that differ from person to person. For example, the fact that I live in a warm, safe home with food in my kitchen is not because I work any harder, am any smarter, or any more deserving than a parent in Indonesia working twelve hours a day just to get food for their children. Two mothers with equal ability, equal responsibility, and the same work ethic but unequal opportunities will lead two very different lives.

Our family has the privilege of sponsoring children through an organization called Compassion.[39] I strongly recommend that if you are looking for a way to create opportunity for someone else, then sponsoring a child is a good way to do it. You can find out more at www. compassion.com.

The minute we start to think we deserve the life we lead, we open the door for pride to creep in, and with it comes all sorts of ugly dinner companions. The fact that I was born in the UK already gives me an educational advantage beyond much of the global population. I live in a country where healthcare is accessible to everyone regardless of income and where the state takes responsibility for ensuring its citizens are cared for. Whether the state is successful or not is a subject for much debate, but even the fact that system exists is a privilege. We are all running the same journey of life. We are all equal in value, yet we start on that road at different places and with different weights to carry.

My question to myself all the time (in fact I wear myself out with this one) is this: Am I doing enough with what I have been given? My parents weren't rich, but we had everything we needed. They were in a very happy marriage, and I went to an average comprehensive school in the UK. I worked hard with what I was in my hands and ended up on a full scholarship at Cambridge University.

With that opportunity comes the responsibility to do something. To make a difference. To be a voice for the voiceless. To improve the starting point for others. To make others' lives a little better. If all I do is use my privilege to accumulate for myself, then I am behaving no better than the toddler who grabs all the toys for themselves, just because they are bigger and faster than the other kids.

Regardless of wealth, social status, nationality, and so on, we all have the same twenty-four hours in a day, the same sixty minutes in each hour. Most of us can choose what we do, and how we spend it. I am not saying to be a martyr and fail to improve your own world. I am asking whether spending our lives in hedonistic pursuit feels a little wasteful if we are also able to make the lives of others' much better as well. I question whether working to only make ourselves happier even works. Perhaps, by pursuing others' happiness, we in turn find ourselves in a better place.

● If Not You, Then Who?

Nik and I have been involved in the charity WeSeeHope since it started in 2000.[40] The charity was founded by husband and wife, Phil and

Wendy Wall. At the time, Southern and Eastern Africa were the regions most affected in the world by HIV and AIDS, and millions of children were being orphaned and made vulnerable as a result.

It was during a visit to South Africa in 1997 that Phil met a little girl called Zodwa, who had been abandoned by her mother. Having failed in their attempt to adopt her, but deeply moved and inspired by their experience, Phil and Wendy decided to take a unique approach to try and help other children like Zodwa. This was their catalyst for change. They invested their personal savings and created an extraordinary fund-raising challenge; they gave people ten pounds and encouraged them to turn it into one hundred pounds using only their talents, passions, and networks to do so. Phil and Wendy's 1010 Challenge raised over £2 million and led to the formation of WeSeeHope. They have now raised over £22.7 million in support of vulnerable children in Southern and Eastern Africa. What a great way to give to others. Phil and Wendy gave away their security and their personal savings to provide security for others. Nik and I are still ambassadors for the charity and do what we can to raise funds and awareness of the marvelous work they do to protect and support vulnerable young people.

I'm not saying everyone needs to start a charity and give all their money away. But we all have time. We all have life. And we are spending it. What are we spending it on? Something we will be pleased to own/to pass on/to be known for? Or something which, in truth, will rot, we can't take with us, will lose its value, or lose its joy?

To find meaning and purpose in life brings an enormous amount of joy. That purpose can be different for everyone. We are not all Mother Teresa. Running a successful business is important work. Creating jobs, a safe place, and provisions for our families matters.

> **What would you be proud to hear at your eulogy?**

144

● Time Famine

Think about what leads you to enjoy life and try to do more of that. Do you need more time? How can you allocate your time differently? Give yourself a break! If your portion is too big, you have two options: either reduce your portion or expand your plate. Which is more doable for you?

Professor Elizabeth Dunn, Professor of Social Psychology at the University of British Columbia (UBC) and a researcher on happiness, presents data that suggests we don't buy ourselves more time even when we could.[41] Research shows people who value time over money tend to be happier. Therefore, why don't we use our precious resource of money to get us something which, according to happiness researchers, will buy us more happiness?

Could you live in a smaller house or take on less responsibility at work? Could you free some time and resources up to make life more enjoyable? You only get to live life once. Your house (and the size of it) will probably remain after you have gone. When you have moved out and moved on, someone else will move in. Your life is not your house.

You may not need to reduce your outgoings or reduce your income in order to find more time. Perhaps you can buy someone else's time to add to yours? What could somebody else do as effectively as you? Could someone else benefit from the work while you benefit from the time?

I realize, of course, there is huge inequality embedded in these questions. Many people require more space and are working all the hours they possibly can to make ends meet. This concept of using money to create more time seems to apply to only the wealthy. But if that applies to you, perhaps you can think of a way where you can use your time differently for your benefit? If you can't afford childcare, can you get creative with friends and pool your resources together? Could you organize a school run schedule? Could you cook double and deliver it to your neighbor one day a week and they do the same for your family, thereby buying each family one evening a week without that food prep?

Where can you get inventive in allocating your time and resources differently? Where can you build community and trust with your neighbors by helping each other out more?

It is interesting in Dunn's research that the wealthy don't always use their money to buy time, either. There are a few different reasons why this may be the case, but one suggestion is the higher economic value their time has. For example, the higher our hourly rate, the more we perceive our time as scarce. People tend to perceive things that are scarce as valuable and things that are valuable as scarce. Therefore, according to Dunn's research, the more you think your time is worth, the more you feel that you don't have enough of it.[42]

One of the ways which you can perceive less "time famine" is by volunteering your time for free. If you want to feel you have more time, give it away for free! I love this, as not only does it help us with our perception of time famine, but it also helps us to help others, and that in turn gives us good feelings. It's like a great meal that looks good, tastes good, and does your body good. Why would you not?

● Standing Order Audit

Are you investing your time, energy, and money into something that was initially important to you, but over time a standing order got set up, and you no longer notice or pay attention to it? Maybe a decision to do something once has taken time, energy, and resources on a regular basis. You may not have agreed to it frequently, but you agreed to do it once or twice, and now, having paid no attention to it, you hardly notice that it is still asking the same of you. Do you need to stop that standing order? If you were to start at the beginning again with your current situation, passions, and resources, would you make the same decision? By not saying no or stopping something, you are effectively saying yes each day, week, month, and year.

I am not suggesting to go back on commitments you made. But look at what you are currently committed to, and be sure it is still for the right reasons. Reassess and be sure you'd still say yes for your today and your tomorrow. If you are not careful, you could start spending your life on something that doesn't matter to you.

Take your "normal" week and write all the things that are demanding your time. Then write "What Does It Matter?" beside them. It may explain your tiredness, boredom, or excitement. It may challenge you on something you spend yourself on that you don't really treasure. It may also remind you of the important things and the things you relish giving your time to.

Days are Numbered

Earthly life is like a bank account that has an unknown spend limit. When you spend a day, you cannot get it back. You cannot relive that day. Today will only happen once. Our days are numbered, we just don't know what that number is!

Make the most of your life and spend it in a way that you will be pleased with according to what matters to you. Don't spend it unthinkingly. That leads to more regrets than necessary. Spend it knowingly. Spend it wisely, spend it joyfully, spend it with excitement and peace. You can only spend it once, so be glad with your purchase.

It may be that to spend your life well, you don't need to do more. You may need to do less. If you believe doing less will help you, then do less well. Do less without guilt. Do less because you are enjoying life. Making the most of hard work already done is part of the fun.

It is not for me to judge how you are spending your life. I am asking you to judge it! Evaluate and assess. Pause and reflect. Be sure you are spending your hours the way you really want to.

What Does It Matter?...
...What I Possess?

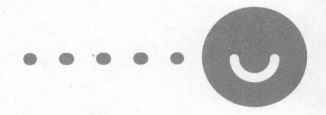

YOURS?

Be a Good Girl

I did not do well with the culture of parenting a toddler. I felt like a giraffe on ice skates. I would consciously take a deep breath and search for courage to walk over the threshold into a room of overtired adults, each struggling to hold a meaningful conversation against the backdrop of tantrums and pandemonium. That was my problem right there; my expectations were for meaningful conversation, when in reality, a parent at a toddler group has succeeded if they managed to arrive at all.

Adults at these groups often inquire of each other how much sleep they're getting, whether they have managed to eat, and how on earth they arrived not only fully dressed but also with their clothes clean. Nevertheless, aside from my hope of conversing, I simply found the noise, chaos, and interruptions really hard to handle. It seemed to be an endless jolt of disturbed conversations and activity. At any time, a parent might be needed to avert catastrophes such as a child eating her own shoe or smashing a tambourine on the head of another tiny human.

A typical incident would be that the treasured plastic car (with roof and door, no less) would suddenly become available as Child A got bored with it and wanted to move on. Welcome Children B and C onto the scene. Noticing that the car was now available, they both pitter-patter as quickly as their little legs could carry them over to the car, and they arrive at the same time to disastrous consequence. Child B was further away to begin with, and Child C had been loitering near the car for just this moment. Child B is bigger and faster, and so distance being somewhat irrelevant, they clash at the door handle with a shriek, a tug, and a stare, confirming the confrontation, to which they are now both fully committed. On hearing the howling, Child A turns around and cannot believe that they were so silly as to leave "their" car unattended for even a moment, and goes back to reclaim their territory, declaring: "Mine, mine, mine," while trying to pull Child B and C away. And there we have it, a classic three-way tug-of-war over a car, all three claiming it as their own and determined to use their wit, strength, and any advantage possible to own it.

Their respective adults would launch themselves across the room at breakneck speed and intervene. Mostly, after a quick look up to see who is watching and how harshly they are being judged, a parent would rebuke their child. Child A would be told off for being selfish. They had their turn, and it was quite right that others should "have their turn." They were admonished and told to share. Child B would be scolded for using their sheer size, strength, and weight to their advantage and would be encouraged to let the "little kid" go first. Child C would be told to stop crying, that it isn't their car, and they have no more rights to it than anyone else.

These rules mostly apply while children are toddlers and also into their school years. There comes a time, though, when suddenly, or perhaps gradually, the same rules no longer seem applicable. I have seen parents get cross their child wasn't picked for the lead role in a production or for the A team at football. I've seen parents working the system to ensure their child has the best chance, regardless of the effect on others. Parents can often fight for their child to have the upper hand. They assume their child is in the right, whatever the child says is true, and that the world is a competition that should be won by their family.

I am bewildered by the undeterminable moment of change between childhood and adulthood, when one behavior, previously admonished, is now acceptable or even worse, applauded and rewarded. What changed?

Paradigm Shift

This subtle reshaping of attitude in some parents also nudges their children down this slope. Children who were once told to share and that they shouldn't use their advantage to push others out of the way now see their parents doing exactly that on their behalf. They observe the rules have changed and feel permission to do the same. That teenager grows into an adult, and hey presto: they behave like a toddler at work and somehow, incredulously, it is endorsed and maybe even acclaimed.

When that adult then has children, they go back to the play group as a parent, admonish their child for being selfish, taking more than their fair share, and for overpowering other children. They lay down rules about not whacking other kids with wooden spoons from the play kitchen, and how each child should "take their turn." They roll their eyes when their kid grabs not only one piece of cake from the tray, but two, one in each clenched fist. They huff and puff when their child rummages through the dress-up box, grabbing what they wanted and leaving a mess of clothes strewn over the floor for someone else to clean up. They train their child to share, to be kind and honest. And so the cycle begins again.

Please don't misunderstand me. Competition is healthy and good. It is an important part of business and life, and I find it fun! There is a difference, though, between healthy competition and a stinking attitude that reeks of selfishness, disregarding the cost to humanity or our planet. Children are told off for telling lies. I wonder how many times adults take part in less-than-honest behavior and convince themselves it's fine. How hypocritical for an adult to punish their child for lying and then do so themselves because, of course, adulthood gives you permission, right?

Was this competitive and selfish behavior at the core of the adults at the playgroup all along? Was it the audience of other adults that brought out the best, and not the worst in them? Do we need an audience for accountability?

Poor behavior reprimanded in a toddler is somehow excused in adult life. Often, it is the same toddler behavior just taking different forms. Rather than fighting over the plastic car, we're now fighting over real ones.

When bulk buying in preparation for quarantine in the UK, the fastest shoppers won. Those who could afford to buy and keep stock won. Those who were able-bodied to get to the shops won. Those who were unable to get there quick enough or who simply couldn't afford to stock up a month's supply lost out. They were left looking at empty shelves, wondering how they were going manage the next few days without the basics they needed.

But when people became aware of the stock crisis, it was wonderful to see so many step up and volunteer their time. It was humanity at its best, serving each other and putting others' needs before their own. It was exciting to witness the power of community when we rallied around the common enemy of the pandemic. It felt good. It felt like those lessons we learned as children were put into practice, and the goodness woven into the fabric of our being got to shine. Able-bodied people became the hands and feet for those who needed it. Food distribution became an urgent matter, and ensuring everyone had their personal "five to thrive" became the most important thing.

We can use our strength to make way for the vulnerable and weak. We can choose not to overpower them to accumulate more for ourselves. Can you think of people who were badly behaved in business and as a result increased their bonuses but decreased their friends and depth of relationships? I have seen many senior leaders who are not only skilled and knowledgeable, but who also care about their people and are empathetic and kind. You don't have to be unkind or thoughtless to achieve success.

We are hardwired for survival, and I am not fighting our biology. To what extent, though, do I prioritize my survival, and to what extent do I prioritize my greed? Interestingly, our biology rewards us for being kind and generous. I'm not saying we shouldn't make business profitable. It is wise to make a profit and grow your business. But let's check we don't trample over other people in the process of making that happen. Surely, if we stop to ask "What Does It Matter?" we will remember that humans are more important than money.

It occurs to me that if a toddler behaved the way a lot of adults do, with the mentality of "Me first, it's mine, I want, no, you can't have it, me first, no I won't share," then those looking on would likely correct them. "Come on now, it's good to share, don't hit, say sorry." My dad used to say, "'I wants' don't get." The things is, these deep-rooted attitudes we admonish in small children do not disappear. We simply become more refined in our demands and how we demonstrate them, more adept at hiding our self-centered way of living. Few issues are as prevalent in this matter as food distribution on our planet. Whole companies and societies choose themselves over their neighbor. We want it at a certain cost, choosing not to see the communities ravaged by our decisions.

Of course, when you are an adult you have more control over your sharing, and that is exactly when we should put our childhood lessons into action. Contrary to the story we tell ourselves, putting us at the center of our lives does not lead to happiness. The media may scream at us to be number one and selfish in a competitive marketplace, but does that really help us?

We love to witness others' altruistic behavior. We celebrate when people are kind and loving, and hold it up as the right way to be. We create awards ceremonies and titles in recognition of other people's goodness. We tear up as the strings play behind the film telling the story of unselfish behavior. There is no doubt that humans have an unbeliev-able capacity for love, courage, kindness, and selfless sacrifice. When we witness the virtue of other people, it makes us feel great.

Greed is not a sexy word. It's not a word I hear often, and being greedy is not an attractive disposition. It has an incense of selfishness, grabbing, get at all costs, and overindulgence. None of which are things I want to be known for. Greedy people in cartoons and films are unat-tractive and mean.

Man in the Mirror?

One of the biggest challenges surrounding greed is that it is easy to see in others and extremely difficult to see in ourselves. We know it is there to some extent, but it is hard to recognize in ourselves. It's a bit like your mouth. You know it's there, but it takes some effort in order to be able to see it. Greed takes some effort to see.

If our behavior was scaled down to toddler size and put in a room with other adults watching, how would we feel? Do we operate on a "me first" system that goes against our training as children? Are we wanting to take what is not ours? Are we willing to share? Are we doing what suits us and leaving behind an untold mess for others to clear up? Are we so engrossed in making our lives comfortable that we have lost sight of the repercussions for future generations?

Hardwired for Love and Generosity

Research shows we are hardwired for love. Hooray! We are hardwired for helping others, and our brains reward us with good feelings when we do. One of the best ways you can feel better about your situation is to take action and help someone else. This is powerful because you both benefit and feel better for that act of compassion. I remember hearing an extremely wealthy celebrity say that the only thing that really brought satisfaction to him was being useful to someone else.[43] How brilliant, because wealth and fame are out of reach for many of us, so if they were the answer to fulfilment, we'd be doomed! But helping others is available to each and every one of us. The good feelings of putting others first are readily accessible. We just need to take action and release ourselves from the "me and mine" echo chamber. By focusing on others' needs, we invariably sate our own desires. I was first introduced to Coralus by a client who had invited me to a drinks reception.[44] As I listened to the founder's vision, I wanted to scream with delight. The phrase "radical generosity" struck a chord with me and their mandate to practice this through sharing capital, resources, and connections was inspiring. They were a group of radically generous people, committed to making the world better for all. It is exciting to see this group giving and sharing in a way that benefits not only themselves, but others as well.

They are not alone. There are countless stories of people and organizations working for the good of others, not just themselves. Growing up, I used to think you could be either profitable or charitable. Now there is a move to be both. Companies are considering not only profit, but also people and the planet. It is exhilarating to witness and feels good to be part of.

● Naked Truth

You were naked once and will be, repeatedly. When you are laid to rest, you may not be naked, but you won't know what you are wearing! You arrive into this world with no possessions, and you can't take any with you. Let that sink in for a minute.

Do you find that reality depressing or freeing? It brings up a mix of emotions in me. First, I don't want to think about dying. I'm not afraid of it. I just like life here on earth right now! Second, it immediately leaves me wondering why I put so much energy into a cycle of earning and buying. For me, purchases and money make life easier and more enjoyable for ourselves and others. If a purchase doesn't do that, then I need to question why I am buying it.

Our age of accumulation bombards us with the message that there should be a consistent increase in the number of things we own, as well as the size, location, or standard of our property. Marketing machines are spewing the lie that we will be happier, healthier, and more fulfilled the more we possess. But wealthy people often disagree, and so does the research.

The Harvard Study of Adult Development may be the longest study of happiness in adult life that's ever been done. In this ongoing study, two groups of men have been tracked since 1938. One group started as participants in the study when they were sophomores at Harvard College, and the other group were boys from Boston's poorest neighborhoods, particularly those from troubled and disadvantaged families. When summarizing the lessons from the lives of these 724 men, psychiatrist Robert Waldinger states that it isn't wealth, fame, or working harder that kept the men happier and healthier. It was good relationships.[45] Those men who leaned into good and healthy relationships with family, friends, and community fared the best. It takes wisdom to ask "What Does It Matter?" when approaching our relationships and purchases.

Have you ever found you bought what you did not need? I know I have. Have you ever asked yourself why? I read a news article recently about the resurgence of car boot sales (similar to yard sales), and it quoted one shopper as saying: "...I even got flippers, for free! I don't even need flippers!" How interesting that we celebrate buying what we do not need. Looking at the smile on the lady's face it was clear she enjoyed the process of treasure hunting and that, for her, it was not a cost but a joy. We are all different, and some people love shopping, while others don't. What interested me was that she recognized, even before leaving the field where she picked the flippers up, that she didn't need them. I wonder if they will simply sit in a wardrobe or under-stairs cupboard somewhere, unused until she herself does a car boot sale and passes them on to someone else? How long will it be before those flippers are used for the purpose for which they were made? A question we could ask before making a purchase is: Will this bring meaning to my life? Or put another way, "What Does It Matter?"

Asking this question will help us see in the moment what matters and what doesn't. It may be that buying that new outfit will absolutely bring you joy in the moment. Great! It may be that demonstrating self-discipline to walk away from the new outfit will give you a sense of control and strength. Great! It may be that we realize the purchase doesn't matter at all and that our finances could be better used elsewhere, creating less strain and stress on our family. Great! It may be that the extravagance of buying that gift for someone brings us so much pleasure that we knowingly exchange some of our savings to savor a moment with someone else.

I remember buying Nik an expensive gift for no reason at all other than I wanted to show him I loved him. It was totally extravagant. There was no birthday or anniversary. It was an ordinary Friday in an ordinary week, but once the idea took hold and I gave myself permission to go for it, I thoroughly enjoyed every second of choosing the gift, getting it wrapped, and taking it home. I was giddy with excitement to give it to him. We happened to have very good friends over for the evening, so I called the room to attention before I looked him in the eye, told him I loved him more and more every day, and presented him with this unexpected, expensive gift. It was the thing romantic comedies are made of. Nik was blown away. We shared the moment and then moved on with our normal Friday night movie. Giving Nik that gift then was worth the five very average items of clothing I may have refused to buy in order to pay for it. They didn't matter enough. This did. He did.

There is a time for frugality and a time for extravagance. If we ask "What Does it Matter?" we may find clarity on which is which. Everything we buy comes at a cost. And it comes at a cost that is more than the price tag displayed to us. It costs us our time and energy. If I were to buy a pair of shoes for fifty pounds, the cost to me would be greater than pounds. The actual cost would also include the time to earn that fifty pounds, the cupboard space I need to store them, the fuel to get to the shops, and the time and energy spent shopping for them.

The beauty of asking "What Does It Matter?" when it comes to spending our money is that everyone's answer will likely be different. The answer will bring wisdom to our thinking, feeling, and behavior in any one moment.

A purchase may have profound meaning. When we purchased my piano, it had significance to me that went far beyond simply having a beautiful instrument in the house. I used some money I had inherited from my grandmother, so it was a gift from her. It also felt like a "coming of age" moment to finally have my own piano in my own home. It brought me freedom to write and play. Since leaving my parents' house, I had been playing a keyboard in my bedroom. This meant that when I played, I needed to go upstairs to my room, turn the power on, and so on. It was a decision to play and practice. Now I had a piano in my living room, lid open, enticing me to play. It felt like it called out my name as I walked past, and I walked past it many, many times a day! Importantly, it was the sound I had been aching for. No matter how good my keyboard had been in my college room, nothing matched the sound of a real piano. Even dusting my piano still evokes memories of my mom cleaning our house. The run of notes up and down the piano as the duster slides over the keyboard reminds me of my childhood. Sometimes, purchases add meaning to your life.

There is a time for extravagance, and a life with no feasting is the poorer for it. I am not exhorting a life of no purchases. I am encouraging you to purchase what matters to you and to do so in the knowledge of its full cost. Marketing machines are clever liars. Be cleverer than they are.

● More Stuff, More Self?

The observation that our self-perception is wrapped up in our possessions or lack thereof is not a new concept. In 1890 William James (who is cited to have founded the psychology department at Harvard) said that if we have been involved in the making or improving of something, it has even more value to us.[46] He also wrote that our depression at the loss of certain goods is not just that we now have to go without them, but that with them departs some level of our true selves. That after the loss of possessions, there is a sense of the shrinkage of our personality. He said if we lose a little of our stuff, we lose a little of ourselves. Do you feel that the idea of less possessions equates somehow to less of you? Advertisements are often designed to make you to feel this way.

The marketing machine wants to sell. We do not always need to buy. Sellers need consumers more than consumers need sellers. I know this to be true from the fact that all I buy is not necessary to my living.

● More or Less?

Sometimes there is pride in choosing less. If we're not careful, a little self-righteous attitude of "we are above the power of purchasing" can come across, and the choice to own less becomes a status symbol all its own. I am not suggesting we no longer shop or enjoy doing so. I am suggesting we should always pause and ask ourselves "What Does It Matter?"

If you need a new pair of shoes, and having those shoes is worth the actual cost of them, great. You have evaluated it and made a decision that works for you, so you can fully enjoy the process and purchase! But when buying them has more to do with your mood than your wardrobe, perhaps take a breath and walk away, even if only for a few hours. Choosing to implement self-discipline this way is vitally important for our well-being. It reminds us that we are in control of our behavior.

Self-discipline is not a popular word. Or rather, "self" is an extremely popular word. Self seems to be an all-consuming concept that demands much of the western world's attention. "Selfies" say it all. It feels like we are more individualistic and more focused on ourselves than ever before. Self is an ever-popular focus of our time and energy. Discipline, not so much. Not because we can't be self-disciplined, but because it requires hard work and resisting immediate gratification. The more we demonstrate self-discipline, the more self-disciplined we become. It is like a muscle we can train.

Immediate gratification culture wants the result but not the discipline to get there. Some of the older generation criticize the younger generation for this impulse, and yet I believe those that have gone before must take some of the responsibility. They are the ones who have perpetuated this ideal lifestyle through advertising and marketing campaigns, lying to the public that if only they had more, they would be happier.

● More Clothes, More Laundry

My laundry is an ever-present struggle to stay on top of because, to be honest, we have more clothes than we need. I can ensure all the clothes we need for the week are in our wardrobes and still find my ironing basket overflowing. There is just too much. In fact, there is simply too much stuff in my house. I'm not a frequent shopper. I'm pretty practical about my purchases. But neither am I a frequent sorter. I love the house to be tidy, and it being messy can leave me feeling overwhelmed. Our busy life can simply accumulate debris around us, and we don't notice the seaweed the tide of a busy rhythm of work and rest can wash ashore. Especially with children. They pick things up from one room, look at it as they carry it to another, and then leave it there! I mean, *why*? I can be tidying one room and feel a sense of achievement from the progress I make, only to look behind and see my kids being "creative."

In these moments I need to ask myself afresh "What Does It Matter?" And the answer is not simple. On one hand, the mess doesn't really matter that much, and I totally get that. There are days when I collapse at the end of the day knowing full well that if I don't leave something undone, I, myself, will be undone!

There are other times, though, when taking control of my environment is supremely helpful in decluttering my mind and emotions at the same time as decluttering the porch. It feels like the sorting and organizing of my home, office, or studio is somehow reflected in the waters of my mind. When I say the answer is complex it's because it is different for us all. We can all tolerate different levels of mess, and actually, many would agree that overly obsessive cleaning is a symptom of something more serious.

> I believe there is a time to clutter and a time to clean. "What Does It Matter?"

I believe the "this is how you do life" message hitting us hard through social media and other channels is unhelpful because we are all unique. There is no one type of human and no one type of "best life."

Tidying up can help you feel more in control and less anxious. As you gain control over your environment, there is a sense of achievement and well-being that feels good. The freedom to not tidy up can also feel powerful. Find the freedom to do it, or find the freedom not to do it. Whatever you do, though, do it consciously and enjoy it. Enjoy the process and the result.

There are differing opinions on this. Marie Kondo, arguably this generation's tidying guru, has created a tidying methodology and industry, implying it is of utmost importance. Her website even suggests that tidying up can have transformational power. I have read articles stating that tidying up and organizing our belongings can be life changing. Getting rid of some of our belongings even more so. On the other hand, Benjamin Franklin was one of the Founding Fathers of the United States and was reported as saying he never managed to be tidy. I'm sure you'll agree that he managed to achieve quite a lot.

The point is, what is good for you may not be right for someone else. Does looking at their perfect house irritate or inspire you? What does it matter to you if your home or desk is tidy? What does it matter to you of it's not? Either way, know the answer for yourself and live with that. It may change. One week I can handle the mess, the next I need to deal with it.

The point is, you are free to choose. If you find yourself repeating the phrase, "I *have* to cook dinner, I *have* to do the laundry, I *have* to…." No, you don't. You actually don't. You could choose to be hungry and smelly. It's your choice. So if you choose to feed yourself, find the joy in it and find gratitude, because it will make everything so much better!

Don't let clearing your environment become yet another burden in an already busy life. Give tidying a go, and if you find it helpful, do it as much as you find it helpful. It's your life. It's your space. It's your time and energy. Learn from others, but remember they are not in charge of you and your possessions. They do not necessarily know you, your motivations, your circumstances, your preferences, character, or capacity. Don't let a social media algorithm dictate what you own or how you spend your life.

If you want to rest, rest. If you want to clear, do that. "What Does It Matter" which you choose? You can choose to tidy or choose to rest and enjoy it. Feel empowered, not burdened by it.

There's a time to tidy and a time to rest.

There is a time to buy and a time to refrain.

There is a time to give and a time to receive.

Stop and ask "What Does It Matter?" to help you figure out what is right for you in any given moment.

What Do I Matter?...

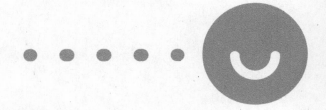

WHAT DO I MATTER?

Compulsory Roller Coaster

The years 2020 and 2021 were extremely challenging for me, both per-sonally and professionally. It wasn't all bad, but like many of you reading this, my business was hit very hard by the pandemic, and I was homes-chooling our children. I was stretched beyond belief and found myself asking "What Does It Matter?" on an hourly basis to help decipher my priorities in an unknown terrain.

I remember splurging this little ditty one morning while trying to keep my spirits high. Choose any silly tune to sing along:

***

Lockdown Working Mother

I'm a lockdown working mother
And my house is in a mess
I feel that I've achieved if I remember to get dressed
I race for logins and downloads, so my kids can go to school
And just as I sit down to work, my gorgeous offspring call...

Lockdown
Gotta juggle work and home
Oh, it's lockdown
Where the heck did I put my phone?
Oh, it's lockdown, normal service won't resume
I delay my morning shower (again), I'm running out of
power (again)
But I need to go and join another Zoom

I could choose to bake a cake
But I don't have any flour
My hair is in a state, it's getting worse by the hour
I don't remember what a handbag is or how to drive a car
But my cupboards sure are cleaner than they've ever
been before (*hey*)

***

Can I hear an "amen" from other lockdown working parents?

I know not all states and countries were in lockdown to the same extent as the UK, but wow—what a roller-coaster ride! It had too many dark tunnels, twists, turns, and anticipatory escalations for my liking. We were locked in, bar across our laps, and catapulted into the distance with no clue what was ahead.

My daughter was about six years old when she experienced her first roller coaster. I remember her giggling as she sat with a friend in the car behind ours. As the ride started to gain momentum, I could hear her bemused voice behind me whispering repeatedly: "I was not expecting this, I was not expecting this, I was not expecting this, I was not expecting this!" with ever increasing volume. The intensity of her exclamations and surprise grew until, at last, the roller coaster came to a sudden stop, and she proclaimed loudly: "I was not expecting that!" That can feel like life sometimes, eh?

I was relieved when the rhythm of our school routine returned, but I knew I required some recovery time. I needed to replenish what I had poured out, so I decided to challenge myself both physically and mentally. I set a goal unlike anything I'd ever done before, and one that would force me to get out of the house. I signed up to run the London Marathon 2021 for WeSeeHope.[47]

● Run, Emma, Run!

I have always enjoyed running. As a teenage girl I chose to get up before 6:30 a.m. to go for a run before the school bus. Yes—madness! My family reluctantly took turns to come with me, as I wasn't yet old enough to head off around the fields on my own. Members of my family responded differently to this call for companionship. I have four sisters, and only two were old enough to come with me. One was eager. One was reluctant every step of the way, and I learned more about coaching than running on those mornings she was with me. My dad was hilarious. He would stop and talk to the horses, sheep, cows, and any living thing in sight to avoid running consistently. He'd chat away with whatever livestock was around, and if it was an empty field, he would find an insect or two to divert his attention so he could catch his breath. We both knew what he was up to, but I absolutely loved the one-to-one time with him, so I never rushed him or felt impatient. It was a pleasure to have his company, even if I shared it with all the livestock in our village.

Even though I loved running, I hadn't run in an organized race since leaving school. I had absolutely no idea what to expect and felt intimidated. I had just enough fear to get me over the threshold of my door on the many occasions I didn't feel like training. I find fear oddly alluring. I like the challenge of a challenge and get bored all too easily if I am faced with something I already know how to do.

I trained diligently and kept to the schedule. I even woke up at 5:15 a.m. while on vacation in Spain to run before it got too hot. I watched the sunrise as I ran, dreaming of a cold shower and ice cream on my return. I get excited by sport, but not everyone does, so I won't bore you with the details, except to say that towards the end of training I was doing long runs of about twenty miles. Nik kept me company on these difficult runs, cycling next to me without complaint. It must have been difficult to cycle for that long at my running speed, but he devotedly kept alongside, feeding me snacks and water. It was a precious time. I had enough breath to chat for the first fourteen miles, but after that I would start to tire. It was then that "Radio Nik" would kick in. He would chat, sing, tell jokes, update me on news, and put the world to rights with only hand gestures (polite ones) from me in response. I loved it. My pace and distance had improved. My eating was controlled. My plan was set. Apart from a slight twinge in my right leg, I was as fit as I'd ever been. I was ready.

Race day was fun. A few others I knew were also running, and an excited support group had promised to cheer us on. It was an amazing atmosphere. The route was lined with people clapping and shouting. Some supporters were jumping up and down, some were cheering from their sofas, having set up house on the pavement. I was glad I'd followed advice and had emblazoned my name on my shirt, because it was fabulous to be encouraged by complete strangers. I was witnessing the best in humanity: runners running for loved ones and causes they felt passionately about against the backdrop of the inspiring crowd. It was fabulous.

As I ran past the 15k sign, I had a moment of revelation. My legs felt as I expected them to feel at 30k. This was the first time I thought I might be in trouble. But I shoved the nagging doubt to the back of my mind, deciding to focus and be OK with the pain searing up my shins. As I passed the half marathon mark at mile thirteen, I started to feel upset. I knew I could complete a half marathon easily, and although my watch displayed a good race time so far, I knew my body was struggling—struggling more than I would have expected. I drew strength knowing my family and friends were waiting somewhere around Canary

Wharf. I just had to keep going until then. I ran, scanning the pavement left to right as I ignored how angry my body was with me.

When I saw my family, I wanted to cry. I ran over and said: "My legs hurt." They cheered me to keep going, to do what I knew in my gut I wanted to do, and I'm so grateful to them for that. One of my sisters (the one who hated running with me on those early mornings before school) even ran alongside me for a few meters: "Come on, Emma. You can do this!"

I continued, thinking that perhaps I had hit "The Wall." I'd heard horror stories of people wanting to give up and had planned how to cope: I would never walk. No matter how slow I got, walking was out of the question. I was gutted, though, that I did end up walking just a little because my legs had started to feel like they weren't really working anymore. I remembered a mantra that a professional marathon runner used, and I said it over and over to myself:

"Sure, it hurts. It's only temporary. Stop your complaining. What's so special about you?" Everyone around me looked exhausted and in pain. I was no different.

As I ran past the London Eye opposite the Embankment, I had a moment of clarity. Both legs weren't hurting the same as each other. In fact, my left leg didn't hurt at all. It was tired, but it didn't hurt. My right leg, on the other hand, was excruciating. My foot stopped working, and I finished my, "oh so good to be challenged" challenge in pain and exhausted. I ran the last mile, which should have been triumphant, feeling very cross with myself that I wasn't enjoying it more. No amount of self-talk helped. "Come on Emma, this is it, you've done it, you're running past Buckingham Palace completing the London Marathon, you did it." I was bewildered. Frustrated that on one hand I was utterly focused, but on the other hand, I was a wobbly wreck.

The running community is a friendly crowd. They were coaxing me on, and one lady even stopped to offer me one of her fizzy cola bottle sweets to burst me through the last mile. I politely declined and gritted my teeth, determined to get to the end. I finally dragged my legs over the finish line and wandered around dazed. Not the glamorous "running over the finish line, waving my hands in the air moment" I had dreamed of at all.

It only took a few minutes to find Nik, and then the reality of what I had achieved sunk in. Hooray! I did it. It felt good. My sisters then did what only sisters could. Right there in Horse Guards Parade on Pall Mall next to Buckingham Palace, they created a human shield around me and stripped me down to my underwear and changed me into warm clothes. I couldn't think straight, let alone figure out which way 'round to put a bra on! When we took my shorts off, I shifted the weight from my left leg to my right, and my leg collapsed underneath me. I was shocked, and realized I was injured, but I was caught up in euphoria and endorphins.[48]

Euphoria and Endorphins

Yes, euphoria and endorphins are the reason I continued to walk to Leicester Square for drinks before walking to Charing Cross Station and getting the train home. Euphoria and endorphins are what enabled me to run, what I now know, was the entire 26.2 miles of the London Marathon 2021...on a broken leg!

I went to hospital later that week and the X-ray showed I had a broken fibula. My leg was traumatized and in a bit of a mess. To the cola bottle lady, if you ever read this, please know I was grateful, but your fizzy fix wasn't enough for my broken leg! The fracture clinic called and told me the X-ray showed the initial stress fracture happened perhaps two or three weeks before the marathon itself. Every mile I ran made the break worse. At around mile twenty-one, I remember stopping and grabbing below my knee. It was probably here that the fracture became particularly bad, and my foot stopped working altogether.

When it became clear I had broken my leg, my overriding desire was to keep it quiet. I didn't want any focus on my injury. I honestly didn't want it to take away from the achievement. I didn't want "the story" to take away from my victory. How silly is that? Family told me it added to the victory and didn't take away from it, but I wanted my attention to stay on the fact that I aimed for the marathon and completed it. The BBC ran a news headline that week of someone else who had done something similar. My leg break was more dramatic, and I was faster. Just saying.

Why did I want to focus on the victory? Why was I batting away the pain? If one of my children had such a painful and swollen leg, I would have taken them to the hospital immediately, not waited four days. I would have taken someone else from the finish line directly to the ER. Why not me?

Why didn't I give myself the same care I give others?

● Message in a Rucksack

It was because the marathon was meant to be my turning point. It was meant to be a line in the sand from where I had been and an indicator of where I was going. This is extremely personal for me to share, but this book is designed to help us all, and there's no point in resisting vulnerability now, so here goes.

When you finish a marathon, you pick up a bag that you packed in advance. If you are sensible, you pack warm clothes, drinks, and snacks. I thought about that finish line and what it meant for me, and I decided to do something I've not done before. I wrote myself a card. I wrote this note to show myself love (which I had been finding hard to do), to celebrate and spark joy (which I had been finding hard to do), and to set my mind on planning a hopeful future (something I had also been finding hard to do).

Here is the card:

It reads:

My girl,

YOU DID IT.

**Things will get better. This finish line is a start line
for your future. There are better days ahead and all
the investment and hard work will not go to waste.**

**I love you and you are worthy of a happy,
fulfilled and purposeful life. You are brave and
strong and others need you to be your full self.
Don't half-live, Emma. Live life to the full. You
know what to do. This finish line is the end of
this season and the start of the new.**

Love you. *x*

WHAT DOES IT MATTER?

When I wrote this to myself, I intended it to be for my eyes only. No one knew I had a little message for myself in my post-race bag. I am sharing it publicly because I wonder if someone reading this needs to replace my name with theirs or write a similar message to themselves.

Finishing on a broken leg was heroic and newsworthy, but it was also heartbreaking and disappointing. I spent the next three months in the house unable to walk or drive. Rather than the springboard of a new start, my marathon training had brought another padlock to my freedom. My very best efforts and all the courage and resilience I could muster hadn't worked. My victory was overshadowed by injury. I wanted to feel hopeful, and instead, I was left in a lot of pain, physically and emotionally.

Do you ever feel that you've done everything right and still things go wrong? Do you feel that you have completed everything within your control and yet you still feel out of control? The adage "even the best laid plans" comes to mind. What do you do when you feel like this? What is your default?

I was on yet another physical and emotional journey to healing. I reached out to a very good friend of mine on the sad days, and I shared the good ones with as many people as I could. I did what was helpful to me, even though I didn't feel like it. I shared the sadness, but only with a few. I celebrated the good moments with as many people as I could. I find this to be a helpful approach to most days.

My first workout post-marathon was for fifteen minutes on a bike at level 1. This was probably less than 5 percent of my pre-marathon fitness level. I could have felt downhearted, but instead, I saw it as starting point. The next day I decided to increase those minutes until I rebuilt my muscle strength enough to enable me to go for a long walk again. I set my mind on rehab. I set my sights on recovery.

> Share the sad with a few and the glad with the many.

Why? Because what other choice did I have? I didn't like my other options. Would I choose to stay on the sofa? To stay in pain? To feel sorry for myself? To lose hope? To wrap myself in a comforting blanket of complaining? No.

This is where asking the right questions is so valuable to us. I could, unthinkingly, just retreat and feel sorry for myself. But because I chose to ask "What Does It Matter?" I chose to lay my options out. I saw them for what they were, and I could choose what I really wanted.

A broken leg was not in my plan! But I needed to do the best with what was in my control. As horrible as it was to be constrained by this broken leg for a few months, it would be worse to be constrained by it for the rest of my life.

It happened. It hurt. My cinematic plan of running over the finish line with my hands above my head, grabbing the note to myself, reading it with tears quietly streaming down my face against a backdrop of jubilation with a symphony orchestra building to a beautiful crescendo did not happen. My life is not a Disney movie. (Unfortunately, as I love those.)

My finish line was painful, but still purposeful.

It hurt, but it was still full of hope.

It didn't go as I thought, but then how much of life really does? What did it matter? I made it. I ran the marathon with a broken heart and a broken leg, and I am the better for it. I don't regret it one bit.

I hope that sharing this story may inspire you to write a note to yourself. What would you say? What would your note say about how much you matter? Could you write a note that expresses love, care, and concern for yourself? Do you matter?

What Are You Saying to Yourself?

To be honest, there is a small voice in my head that repeatedly says, "I don't matter." Sometimes I even catch myself saying it out loud. This is appalling and humbling to admit, but it is true. It is the one thought that I wrestle with on a weekly, if not daily basis. Unfortunately, when I am in one of these thinking cycles, I've reached my verdict. Regrettably, I then go about my day collating evidence to prove my verdict true.

This is, of course, the completely wrong way around. Surely we should look at the evidence of our lives and conclude the truth from facts? But no, too often I listen to my own thinking, which is attached to my feelings, and then I scour, twist, and search for evidence to prove my assumption true. How deflating.

When else do we pronounce the verdict and then go about collating evidence to support it? Surely that's the job of the prosecution, isn't it? I fear that, all too often, I behave as my own prosecutor. Often when I think I don't matter, feelings of self-pity, selfishness, and pride are attached to that thinking. I'm embarrassed to say it leads to feelings that often lead to actions of which I am not proud. This is hard for me to confess.

When I notice I am thinking, feeling, and behaving in this way, I catch hold of my thoughts and bring them captive to the truth. I can't let my emotions stomp all over me, wreaking havoc and seeding unnecessary suffering. I refuse to plant a forest of fury, and I don't want to get stuck because I threw an anchor of anger. I will rage against the anesthetic of apathy and will drown out the voice of despair. I will battle my thoughts and win, because I do matter, and every little win changes things. Every little victory sets the scene for the next battle, and eventually, I will win the war.

I know the fight is on many levels and comes in many guises. For me, it is often down to my security and worth. What is your battle? Where is your weakness? Where does your armor have a hole that your thoughts keep penetrating again and again?

I grab hold of unhelpful thoughts and replace them with right thinking. I remind my soul of its worth. I remind my mind how to behave and direct my brain to be helpful to both myself and others around me. I choose to control my thinking, so my thinking does not control me, because my thoughts are not always accurate. My feelings are not facts. To behave as if they were would be foolish and would lead to a life riddled with mayhem and disappointment.

I think on what I know to be true. I ponder on peace. I look at the lovely. I name my blessings, concentrate my efforts on the community that supports me, cherish those around me, and remember I am made in the image of God. He made me and said what He had made was good. Who am I to disagree? I am brilliantly made. My body is amazing, and my mind is outrageously clever. My brain is telling my body to breathe today, and I'm so good at it I hardly notice. In fact, last night I did it with my eyes shut! My heart is loving and kind. I am loved and I love. I am valuable. I matter. How about you?

Even as I write this, I can feel hope stirring in me for myself and you. Perhaps read this next section out loud:

> I matter.
> I am worthy of love.
> I am worthy of success.
> I am worthy of goodness.

I believe there is good and evil. I believe in things unseen. I believe there is a God who loves me and a Savior who died for me. And that truth, ultimately, answers my toxic and disgusting dialogue of "I don't matter" with the response that in fact, I *really* matter. How about you? How do you combat your stinking thinking?

My statement of "I don't matter" is not really a statement. It's secretly a question begging for someone to reach out and answer: "Do I matter?" "Does my life matter?" To ask these questions is human and inevitable. Sensible, even.

If this life on earth is the only permanence you believe in, and you don't believe in life after death, use it well. If you do believe in life after death, still use this life well.

For some, living this life in anticipation of the next is paramount. For others, it is using this life well because they believe this is all they've got. Either way, knowing what matters to you and what you believe is core to living a life you won't regret. What do you believe? What do our lives matter while on this planet? Ultimately, what does it all matter?

I am seeking to make decisions and live my life in line with what I believe truly matters. If I waste my precious breath on angst over something that doesn't matter, then I am foolish and emotional, not sensible. Surely our response to a situation should be equal to the importance of it, or else we may as well spend $1,000 on a bowl of custard and throw a priceless diamond in the trash can.

When leading choirs, my aim is often to make many voices sound as one. One of the things I repeatedly say is that "everyone is a somebody and everyone is a nobody." I mean this is the kindest of ways. If you sing in one of my choirs, your voice is important. You contribute to the sound, and what you do or don't do really matters. On the other hand, if I am distracted by you, and you want to draw all the attention to yourself, choosing not to blend with other singers, then we have a problem. Singing in a choir is a lesson in both confidence and humility. We matter, but not at the expense of others.

Confidence clothed with humility.

Cancer Scare

While writing this book, I was awaiting results to find out if I had cancer. Specifically, the same cancer that killed my mom at a young age. It was a sobering week of contemplation and reflection. It demanded mental fortitude, and I got through it by meditating on scripture, praying, and singing. It forced me to question how I had spent my time. The potential diagnosis at the same time as writing this book intensified my examination on whether I was pleased with the decisions I had made. The honest answer was yes.

It would have been easy to have resented prioritizing family over achievement, people over profit, and spiritual enlightenment over materialism. Instead, I realized how genuinely satisfied I felt when reflecting on these choices. When faced with the question of how I have spent my life and what the next season may look like, I could truthfully say I was pleased. I was devastated because I didn't want to lose the life I had. I didn't want to leave my family and didn't want them to suffer the pain of grief. But I was also pleased I had no major regrets.

I think this one question of "What Does It Matter" is partly responsible for guiding me to a life I am happy with. It has steered me right on many occasions. It has reduced my stress levels and helped me put life into perspective with both the little and large things.

When faced with this massive battle of an unknown, potentially life-ending diagnosis, I asked myself once again "What Does It Matter?" I reflected on the choices I'd made, and they made me feel good because they had benefitted other people and had given me much to be happy about in the process. I saw that even though prioritizing my family over my business had been difficult, I didn't regret it for one second. My business suddenly seemed totally trivial in comparison to just simply wanting to survive, wanting to grow old with my husband, and see my children into adulthood. Nothing else mattered more than that. I wanted to be there for them. I wanted to grow old.

I asked myself whether the world is a better place for me having been here. Would I leave it better than when I arrived? How would my husband cope? How had I set my children up to thrive in life and succeed in finding contentment and contributing to others? This traumatic waiting period caused me to stop and reflect at an even deeper level than I usually do, and my passion and honest desire to keep living to be around my family was my overriding thought. I didn't care about what house we lived in, what job I did, or what letters were after my name.

I simply wanted to live.
I wanted to be healthy and alive.
I had no regrets and much to be grateful for.

The test results came back, and I found myself weeping on my bedroom floor that the worst-case scenario was not in front of me. I had been given the "all clear." My doctor was elated to tell me the results, and I was delighted, though slightly numb in receiving them. It took several hours to actually feel that I had a future ahead of me again.

So, What Does It Matter?

When we face our mortality, what matters comes into sharp and glorious focus. I pray you ask "What Does It Matter?" and that your answer will match the story of your life. Maybe this phrase will help to keep us on the straight and narrow, or even better, the wild and free. Perhaps it will hold us accountable, so we live life with things and relationships in their correct order. To live in a way that means we will have fewer regrets and more joy as we live this incredible life we've been given to live. Every day is gift.

You are amazing! You are skillfully designed, and you have a unique contribution to make to the world. No one else sees the world through your eyes. No one else has walked the same steps, spoken the same words, or experienced the same adventure as you. You are gifted and creative. Leave some things undone, or you yourself will be undone. Give yourself a break before you break. Be patient when you're not OK and choose not to stay that way. Be a problem solver, not problem maker. Be a peacemaker, not troublemaker. Bring calm to those in distress and bring distress to the indifferent. Shout for those who can't speak and listen to those struggling to be heard. Embrace the defensive ones and defend the weak. Show compassion to the needy and resist the greedy. Grow into a better version of you each day, not because others require it, but because you deserve it. You deserve to speak well of yourself, you deserve to take care of yourself, and you are in charge of you.

Each breath is a passing moment we cannot get back. Our lives are a tiny speck on the timeline of humanity. May we all leave a mark of love, joy, and compassion, and may we all leave the world a better place than when we arrived.

Remember to ask "What Does It Matter?" and have the courage to act on your answer, because this life is yours and yours alone. Be true to who you are, what matters to you, and enjoy your day!

**Please visit emmapears.com to access additional
resources related to this book.**

———

Continue the conversation with me:
@emma_pears
emmapears.com

———

If you enjoyed this book, please review it and recommend it.
Your opinion matters!
Thank you.

ACKNOWLEDGMENTS

Many people have contributed their expertise to get this book over the start and finish lines and I want to make special mention of Carlos Darby, Tim Moore, Douglas Hardy, and Gary June (Hardy, June & Moore). Thank you to my editor Debra Englander, and to Heather King and the team at Post Hill Press. Your and skill and patience have been invaluable! I also want to thank Jeb Hogg, Lloyd Kinsley, Matthew Child, Fiona Murden, and Del Manning for your influence, wisdom, creativity, and contribution. This book is so much better for having had you involved.

Special thanks to my Dad, Paul Hunt, for being my trusted first reader and unofficial editor. You are brilliant and your grammar is far better than mine! Thank you for laughing and crying with me as I committed to paper some of the lessons you and Mum taught me. Thank you to Jane for making Dad happy and for the love and support you show us all. I am grateful to my sisters Lou, Sarah, Becky, and Jen, and to all of the people they love most. You are a foundational part of my story and you have contributed deeply to who I am, and the message of this book. I love you.

Thank you to my Nik for allowing me to share some of our story. You are handsome, hilarious, and kind. I adore you and I love living life with you. This book would not exist without you, darling. To Josiah and Jessica, I love you so much. You have both changed my life for the better.

I also want to honour Rik and Chris Pears whom I love very much. I couldn't have done this without you. Thank you for embracing me into your family and always going the extra mile to care for me. It was worth marrying Nik, just to get the two of you! To the Spencer family, thank you for going out of your way to show me love and for acting on what matters most. I love you and I am grateful we are family.

Thank you to Jenny Wolny who has worked diligently and faithfully with me for years, I would not be where I am without you. I know working with me can be a rollercoaster ride, so thank you for holding on! Lyndsay, thank you for the snacks, help, and encouragement to get this project off the ground, we did it! Sylvia, you have walked with me from the very start, thank you! Steve and Rachel Cole, thank you for cheering me on with everything from prayers to hot dinners. Aril, Aina, and our Norwegian family, thank you for your encouragement and wisdom, I love you guys!

Finally, my grateful thanks to you, dear reader, for allowing me to ask you questions. I do not profess to have a perfect and stress-free life. Nor am I here to shout at you and tell you what you should or shouldn't do. I simply wanted us to consider, together, what matters to us and how we might live with less stress and more joy. Thank you for the conversation.

ENDNOTES

1   "Overview: MRI Scan," NHS, accessed August 8, 2022, https://www.nhs.uk/conditions/mri-scan/.

2   Malcolm Gladwell, "On Spaghetti Sauce," TED Talks, July 2013, https://youtu.be/VkhFh5Ms1vc.

3   Mind Genomics is a scientific method used for cognitive analysis. Using cross-segmentation when gathering data gives true data based on people's behaviors, rather than what they think is true.

4   Malcolm Gladwell, "Choice, happiness and spaghetti sauce," TED Talks, 2004, https://www.ted.com/Talks/Malcolm_gladwell_choice_happiness_and_spaghetti_sauce/Transcript.

5   Dr. Caroline Leaf, "Why do we keep making wrong decisions? + Tips to help you become an expert decision maker," *Cleaning Up Your Mental Mess*, Episode 98, October 2, 2019, https://anchor.fm/cleaningupthementalmess/episodes/Episode-98-Why-do-we-keep-making-wrong-decisions---Tips-to-help-you-become-an-expert-decision-maker-eejdds

6   Dr Caroline Leaf, "Why do we keep making wrong decisions? + Tips to help you become an expert decision maker," *Cleaning Up Your Mental Mess*, Episode 98, October 2, 2019, https://anchor.fm/cleaningupthementalmess/episodes/Episode-98-Why-do-we-keep-making-wrong-decisions---Tips-to-help-you-become-an-expert-decision-maker-eejdds

7   Robert Waldinger, "Robert Waldinger: What makes a good life? Lessons from the longest study on happiness | TED," TED Talks, January 2016, https://www.youtube.com/watch?v=8KkKuTCFvzI.

8   Dan Gilbert, "The surprising science of happiness | Dan Gilbert," Youtube.com, April 2012, https://www.youtube.com/watch?v=4q1dgn_C0AU.

9   Dan Gilbert, "The surprising science of happiness | Dan Gilbert," Youtube.com, April 2012, https://www.youtube.com/watch?v=4q1dgn_C0AU.

10 Brehm, J. W. "Postdecision changes in the desirability of alternatives," *The Journal of Abnormal and Social Psychology, 52*(3), 384–389 (1956). https://doi.org/10.1037/h0041006

[11] To put this into context, we were in the Caucasus Mountains in June, 1999, and the Second Chechen War broke out August, 1999.

[12] Psalm 23:1–3 (NIV).

[13] Steven Furtick is the pastor of Elevation Church, https://elevationchurch.org.

[14] Kahneman, Daniel. *Thinking, Fast and Slow*. Farrar, Straus and Giroux, 2013.

[15] Carla Hall, "The Ongoing Call of Remembrance," *The Washington Post*, May 7, 1986, https://www.washingtonpost.com/archive/lifestyle/1986/05/07/the-ongoing-call-of-remembrance/8acec791-cecf-4dda-8b3f-aec72ceeee5b/.

[16] Eva Kor, "The Holocaust twin who forgave the Nazis," *BBC Ideas*, February 2020, https://www.bbc.co.uk/ideas/videos/the-holocaust-twin-who-forgave-the-nazis/p0837wjy.

[17] Wilson, T., Reinhard, D., Westgate, E., Gilbert, D., Ellerbeck, N., Hahn, C., Brown, C. and Shaked, A., 2014. Just think: The challenges of the disengaged mind. *Science*, 345(6192), pp.75-77.

[18] Wilson, T., Reinhard, D., Westgate, E., Gilbert, D., Ellerbeck, N., Hahn, C., Brown, C. and Shaked, A., 2014. Just think: The challenges of the disengaged mind. *Science*, 345(6192), pp.75-77.

[19] Amy Morin, "5 Ways to Stop Reliving Painful Memories," *Psychology Today*, February 28, 2016, https://www.psychologytoday.com/gb/blog/what-mentally-strong-people-dont-do/201602/5-ways-stop-reliving-painful-memories.

[20] Amy Morin, "5 Ways to Stop Reliving Painful Memories," *Psychology Today*, February 28, 2016, https://www.psychologytoday.com/gb/blog/what-mentally-strong-people-dont-do/201602/5-ways-stop-reliving-painful-memories

[21] Ethan Kross, "Calming the voice in our head: Ethan Kross," *Don't Tell Me The Score*, January 2021, https://www.bbc.co.uk/programmes/p0958dyt.

[22] Kross, Ethan. *Chatter: The Voice in Our Head, Why It Matters, and How to Harness It*. Crown, 2021.

[23] Ethan Kross, "Calming the voice in our head: Ethan Kross," *Don't Tell Me The Score*, January 2021, https://www.bbc.co.uk/programmes/p0958dyt.

[24] Inspired by a story told by Timothy Keller.

[25] Dweck, Carol. *Mindset: How You Can Fulfil Your Potential*. London: Robinson Publishing, 2012.

[26] TMO is the Television Match Official.

[27] Dr Joan Rosenberg, "Emotional Mastery: The Gifted Wisdom of Unpleasant Feelings | Dr Joan Rosenberg | TEDxSantaBarbara," Youtube.com, September 2016, https://www.youtube.com/watch?v=EKy19WzkPxE.

[28] Vasundhara Sawhney, "It's Okay to Not Be Okay," *Harvard Business Review*, November 10, 2020, https://hbr.org/2020/11/its-okay-to-not-be-okay.

[29] The Prisons, "The Prisons Video Trust Terry Waite Interview Part 1 of 2," Youtube.com, December 4, 2009, https://www.youtube.com/watch?v=UWvU5o2Axds.

[30] Amy Morin, "The Secret of Becoming Mentally Strong | Amy Morin | TEDxOcala," TEDx Talks, Youtube.com, December 2015. https://www.youtube.com/watch?v=TFbv757kup4.

[31] "Preemptive Love," accessed February 2022, https://preemptivelove.org.

[32] Paul Slovic, "Human Tragedies: The more who die, the less we care | Paul Slovic | TEDxKakumaCamp," TEDx Talks, Youtube.com, July 2018, https://www.youtube.com/watch?v=zIt-THEbNIE.

[33] Paul Slovic, "Human Tragedies: The more who die, the less we care | Paul Slovic | TEDxKakumaCamp," TEDx Talks, Youtube.com, July 2018, https://www.youtube.com/watch?v=zIt-THEbNIE.

[34] US Holocaust Memorial Museum, "Thomas Buergenthal discusses quote from Abel Herzberg," Holocaust Encyclopedia, February 2, 2022, https://encyclopedia.ushmm.org/content/en/oral-history/thomas-buergenthal-discusses-quote-from-abel-herzberg.

[35] Paul Slovic, "Human Tragedies: The more who die, the less we care | Paul Slovic | TEDxKakumaCamp," TEDx Talks, Youtube.com, July 2018, https://www.youtube.com/watch?v=zIt-THEbNIE.

[36] Steve Backshall, "Steve Backshall, Explorer," *Desert Island Discs*, BBC Radio 4, August 2020, https://www.bbc.co.uk/programmes/m000ldlw.

[37] "Winston Churchill Quotes," *Brainyquote*, 2022. https://www.brainyquote.com/quotes/winston_churchill_156903.

[38] I can't remember who said this to me, but I have a feeling it was Phil Wall MBE, who mentored me through my early twenties.

[39] "Compassion UK | Releasing Children From Poverty In Jesus' Name," accessed 2022, https://www.compassionuk.org.

[40] "Weseehope | Skills For Sustainable Futures," accessed 2022, https://www.weseehope.org.uk.

[41] Elizabeth Dunn, "What Is Your Time Really Worth? | Elizabeth Dunn | Tedxcoloradosprings," TedX Talks, Youtube.com, https://youtu.be/ItwFMv-u2YE.

[42] Elizabeth Dunn, "What Is Your Time Really Worth? | Elizabeth Dunn | Tedxcoloradosprings," TedX Talks, Youtube.com, https://youtu.be/ItwFMv-u2YE.

[43] It is important to note here that there is a difference between abundance and necessity. Abundance is something that is more than necessary. We all need to have our basic requirements met, and celebrities who say that possessions don't bring happiness probably have those basic things in place. The possessions and resources they are likely referring to are beyond their needs. They are probably talking about their abundance.

[44] "Coralus," accessed 2022, https://www.coralus.org.

[45] Robert Waldinger, "Robert Waldinger: What makes a good life? Lessons from the longest study on happiness | TED," TED Talks, Youtube.com, January 2016, https://www.youtube.com/watch?v=8KkKuTCFvzI.

[46] James, William. *The Principles Of Psychology*. 2 Vols. (American Science Series, Advance Course.) New York, Holt. 8°". *Science* ns-16 (401): 207–208 (1890). doi:10.1126/science.ns-16.401.207-b.

47 "Weseehope | Skills For Sustainable Futures," accessed 2022, https://www.weseehope.org.uk.

48 *Endorphins can also release stress and create a feeling of well-being.*

Endorphins are the body's natural painkillers. Endorphins are released by the hypothalamus and pituitary gland in response to pain or stress. This group of peptide hormones both relieve pain and create a general feeling of well-being. The name of these hormones comes from the term "endogenous morphine." "Endogenous" because they're produced in our bodies. Morphine refers to the opioid painkiller whose actions they mimic. About twenty different types of endorphins exist. The best studied of these is beta-endorphin, which is the one associated with the runner's high. We also release endorphins when we laugh, fall in love, have sex, and even eat a delicious meal.

"Endorphins: The brain's natural pain reliever," *Harvard Health Publishing*, July 2021, https://www.health.harvard.edu/mind-and-mood/endorphins-the-brains-natural-pain-reliever.